AN ACTOR'S ACTOR

ADVANCE PRAISE FOR THE BOOK

'At last, a biography of Sanjeev Kumar, one of the finest actors in the history of Hindi cinema. This labour of love by Hanif Zaveri and Sumant Batra is a welcome addition to the corpus of writing on the Hindi cinema of yore'—Rahul Rawail, film-maker

'I knew Hari-bhai as an actor and a friend. Rich in insightful details, this biography will hopefully introduce Sanjeev Kumar to a new generation of readers and lovers of Hindi cinema'—Jayshree T., actor

'What a pleasure to come across this warm biography. I wonder why there has been no book on this most brilliant actor and lovable human being so far. I was privileged to direct him in *Sawaal*. Sumant Batra and Hanif Zaveri deserve our gratitude for this much-needed account'—Ramesh Talwar, film-maker

'I have very fond memories of Sanjeev Kumar from the time we acted in *Dastak*. Despite being a star, he never had any airs about himself and would always help his co-stars. This wonderful biography brings to life a forgotten star and a lost era of Hindi cinema'—Rehana Sultan, actor

'In an era of PR-driven celeb bios, this account of one of Hindi cinema's most-loved stars comes across as a breath of fresh air, not to mention that it addresses a void that needed to be filled. It is remarkable that it has taken all this time for someone to write on the life and times of Sanjeev Kumar. This unpretentious, straight-from-the-heart homage to the late actor should be on the reading list of everyone who loves Hindi cinema'—Anita Padhye, author

AN ACTOR'S ACTOR

THE AUTHORIZED BIOGRAPHY OF

SANJEEV KUMAR

HANIF ZAVERI
SUMANT BATRA

FOREWORD BY SHATRUGHAN SINHA

EBURY
PRESS

An imprint of Penguin Random House

EBURY PRESS

USA | Canada | UK | Ireland | Australia
New Zealand | India | South Africa | China | Singapore

Ebury Press is part of the Penguin Random House group of companies
whose addresses can be found at global.penguinrandomhouse.com

Published by Penguin Random House India Pvt. Ltd
4th Floor, Capital Tower 1, MG Road,
Gurugram 122 002, Haryana, India

Penguin
Random House
India

First published in Ebury Press by Penguin Random House India 2021

Copyright © Hanif Zaveri and Sumant Batra 2021
Foreword copyright © Shatrughan Sinha 2021

ISBN 9780670096084

Typeset in Adobe Garamond Pro by Manipal Technologies Limited, Manipal
Printed at Replika Press Pvt. Ltd, India

www.penguin.co.in

This is a legitimate digitally printed version of the book and therefore might not
have certain extra finishing on the cover.

Contents

Foreword by Shatrughan Sinha   vii

Author's Note   xi

Co-author's Note   xvii

1. The Jariwalas   1
2. Hard Times   6
3. Hansuya   13
4. Foray into Acting   17
5. Valuable Lessons   29
6. Jamnadas's Sunghursh   42
7. Love, or Something like It   48
8. The Big Break . . . Success at Last   55
9. *Love and God*: Forever in the Making   63
10. Ways of the Heart   72
11. A Versatile Actor   83
12. A Legendary Rivalry   87
13. A New Day   93
14. Meeting Suchitra Sen   96

15. The Landmark Films   101

16. Two Deaths That Changed Him   127

17. Off-Screen Hero   131

18. Life After the Heart Attacks   149

19. The Final Farewell   161

20. The Last Will and Testament   171

21. *Love and God*: Art vs Fate   177

22. The Last Movie: *Professor Ki Padosan*   181

Awards Won by Sanjeev Kumar   187

Filmography   189

Interviews Conducted by the Authors   211

List of Sources   217

Foreword

'Thou wert my guide, philosopher, and friend!'
—Alexander Pope, English poet

On 6 November 1985, when the call came to Chandivali studio, where I was shooting, I rushed to the second-floor apartment in Bandra, where I'd been welcomed so often with warmth and camaraderie even when I was a newcomer.

On the drive, it was tough to reconcile myself to the thought that my one true friend, philosopher and guide was never again going to give me his wise counsel or his unstinting companionship.

It is true that Sanjeev Kumar had suffered a couple of heart attacks before 6 November. But the stories that whirled around—about him having a death wish, and drinking and smoking himself to death—were untrue. After he'd been operated upon in the US, when I was there on a visit, I flew specially to Houston to see him and to spend some time with him. It was a slim Sanjeev Kumar that I met that day—he had lost much weight. Thereafter, when he returned to India, he quit smoking. He'd also drastically cut down on his drinking. He was taking care of himself, which made his death tragic and unexpected for me. It was an unfortunate genetic, hereditary condition that did him in. All the men in his family—his father, his brothers and he himself—passed away before they could hit fifty.

En route to his house, I recalled precious moments spent with him. Many years later, I recounted an incident in my biography *Anything but Khamosh*, written by Bharathi S. Pradhan. It was one of the many incidents that flashed before me when I was speeding down to his house on 6 November. I remembered how, when I had once needed some money very desperately for a personal reason and some best friends had turned me down after promising it to me, Sanjeev Kumar had quietly sent his secretary, Jamnadas-ji, to see me. Jamnadas-ji had carried with him what looked like video cassettes wrapped up in newspaper but turned out to be wads of currency notes that Sanjeevbhai had sent across. Unlike other acquaintances who talked of interest and terms of credit, Sanjeev Kumar lent me the money without a rupee as interest and on 'returnable when able' terms. To this day, I'm not even sure if I returned the entire amount of money, which I paid back in spurts.

We had much in common. He was born on 9 July. Promi (my wife, Poonam Sinha) and I got married on 9 July, and, of course, he was with us at the celebrations. Another common factor was that we were both notorious latecomers. We were renowned as 'Late Lateefs'. But if I reached the studios late, he fetched up even later.

We did many films together, including *Khilona* (1970). How could I ever forget that Sanjeev Kumar used to carry reels of my student film at the Film and Television Institute of India (FTII) to introduce producers to this 'new boy in town'? He had tried to get me into *Khilona* too, though it was ultimately Mumtaz's adamant stand that really got me that career-making film.

One day, tired of our tardiness during the filming of *Khilona*, the late and great L.V. Prasad told me, 'Since Sanjeev Kumar and you are such good friends, you go to his place and bring him with you. At least that way he will be on the sets on time.' But when I would reach his second-floor flat, I would find Sanjeevbhai still relaxing with his tea and cigarette. He would say, 'We'll leave in a while,' and ask me to relax and have some chai. He was the hero of the film and I an absolute newcomer. But with such 'encouragement', I began to reach the sets even later than usual. *Neem pe karela.*

Every day, the two of us would come up with a new excuse for turning up late. One day we would tell L.V. Prasad, 'Today, there was a bus accident at Mahim Church.' The next day, it would be, 'Two taxis had collided outside Mahim Church.' An exasperated L.V. Prasad finally told us, 'If you can't change the situation, at least change the location. Otherwise, whatever's happening every day is always outside Mahim Church.'

Those were such fun, hilarious times.

When my car reached Pali Hill, I ran up the steps, but it was too late. Sanjeevbhai was no more, and I stood numbly against the wall, looking at his body constantly for eight to ten hours. I don't think I've ever stood in one place for so long in my life, but I was stunned and in sorrow. He was embalmed in front of me, and I followed his body to his funeral.

My wife fainted that day. It was a personal loss for her as well. Whenever she and I fought, as couples are wont to do, and she would cry or threaten to leave me, the only place she would think of going to was 'Sanjeevbhai's place'. She considered him her guardian and placed all her emotional trust in him. Though many people called him Haribhai, till the end both of us called him Sanjeevbhai, because we only got to know him after he had become Sanjeev Kumar. So I didn't want to resort to the filmi familiarity of calling him Haribhai. However, as Rabindranath Tagore said, 'The depth of friendship does not depend on the length of acquaintance.'

I still miss him, my whole family does. He was my sons'—Luv and Kush's—favourite mama.

I do accept that the show must go on. But when I look at the show around me today, at the vast world of entertainment that has opened up, I can't help but feel wistful at how invaluable his contribution would have been to the wealth of feature films, Web series and short films that are currently being made.

Yes, the show must go on and it has gone on. But without Sanjeev Kumar, the show is not what it could have been, would have been and should have been.

Mumbai   Shatrughan Sinha
March 2021

Author's Note

It has been over thirty-five years since Sanjeev Kumar breathed his last, and it is surprising that no one has yet written a biography of the actor. Over the last few years, there has been a renewed interest in the life and times of Hindi film stars of the 1960s and '70s, and yet most of the material that has appeared on him has been in the nature of blogs and magazine articles.

Being a film journalist, I met Sanjeev Kumar on many occasions. My first encounter with him was rather interesting. Between 1977 and 1987, I was an active member of Indian People's Theatre Association (IPTA) as an actor. In 1983, director Ramesh Talwar cast me in a small role in his new Hindi play *Lok Katha*, an adaptation of a Marathi play by Ratnakar Matkari. It opened on 18 June 1983 at Prithvi Theatre, Juhu, with two shows at 6 p.m. and 9 p.m. When the second show was over, around 11 p.m., Ramesh Talwar entered from the left wing of the stage and asked us to wait on the stage with our costumes and make-up on. We thought he wanted to click some photographs for the media. All of us—Lubna Siddiqui, Sudhir Pandey, Mustaque Khan, Ashok Pandit, Raj Verma, Sudesh Berry and others—sat on the floor. Suddenly Sanjeev Kumar entered from the left wing with Ramesh Talwar. He sat down on the floor with the rest of us. He was our senior who had started his acting career with the IPTA. So, he always made it a point to attend IPTA's new plays.

Once the group photo was done, I rushed to the make-up room to change my costume. Emerging from it and going down the stairs, I saw Sanjeev standing with A.K. Hangal near the stage wing, cracking jokes and laughing. He saw me and offered his right hand to shake. '*Aap ka kaam achchha tha, dil laga kar karte rahna* (You have done a good job. Keep working hard).' I was amazed to hear the compliment, because I had played a very small role and hardly had three dialogues to deliver in the whole play.

I asked him, 'Sir, my role was too small. How did you recognize me?'

He replied, 'So what? A role is a role. You played a farmer's role, who witnesses a rape with two other farmers, right?'

Before our conversation could continue, Mr Hangal introduced me to Sanjeev. 'Hari [as Sanjeev Kumar was called], he is a freelance film journalist, Hanif Zaveri.'

The moment he heard my surname, Zaveri, he asked me in Gujarati, '*Tamey Gujarati chho* (Are you Gujarati)?'

Sanjeev Kumar was the first person from the Jariwala family to enter films. He had no godfather in the industry and made it on his own steam. He started off with small roles in plays. The first time his name appeared in a newspaper was in the eveninger *Bulletin*, where his performance in IPTA's play *Ward No. 6*, directed by R.M. Singh, was heralded with the headline 'Histrionic Talent Born'. He began his film career with C-grade stunt films. In Hindi cinema, if you start with C-grade films, it is almost impossible to get a chance in an A-grade film. Sanjeev defied all the typecasting that went with being part of lowbrow films and made it to the top bracket.

I was a fan of Sanjeev Kumar. So, I told him that I wanted to interview him. He gave me his landline telephone numbers and asked me to contact Mr Jamnadas for an appointment. And within a week I was at Chandivali studio for my first interview with him.

During my interactions with him, I discovered that he had an amazing sense of humour. He had no qualms about making fun of himself. I observed how as an actor he was not entirely bound by the script. He understood the demands of the scene and added his own bit to improve it. He was a director's actor. Though he seldom discussed a scene with his co-stars, he was always cooperative and helpful when they needed his advice or during rehearsals. He was always aware about his continuity scene and other aspects of the film. He once narrated his experience of shooting for Yash Chopra's *Trishul* at the Rajkamal Kalamandir studio (Parel). As the director shouted 'camera roll, start sound, clap, action', Sanjeev began his dialogue and immediately said, 'Cut it.' Yash Chopra was taken aback and asked, 'Hari, what is wrong?' Sanjeev replied, 'Yashji, yesterday, when we shot this scene with Mr Amitabh Bachchan, my cigar was half, and now I have been given a new cigar. So before starting I should smoke half of it.' This demonstrates his attention to the minutiae of film-making.

Very few people know that at a young age Sanjeev Kumar played the role of an old man in IPTA's play *Damru*, an adaptation of the Telugu play *Bhayam*. It was directed by A.K. Hangal. While watching the play, Prithviraj Kapoor didn't realize that a young boy was playing the role of an old man. Inexperienced as he was, Sanjeev Kumar felt that Hangal had not done justice to him by giving him the role of an old man. So, one day he asked Hangal, 'You know I am young . . . Why did you cast me in the old man's role? Who is going to accept me as a young hero after watching this play?' Hangal explained to him, 'If I had given you the role of the young hero, you would be a hero forever. You would never be an actor. The life of an actor is longer than that of a hero. A good actor always sees the potential of the role, not its length or the age of the character.' Sanjeev kept this in mind forever.

At one time he was playing the role of Jaya Bhaduri's husband in Gulzar's *Koshish*, while playing the role of her father in *Parichay*— both films released within a short period of time, in 1972. In May

1973, he did one more film as hero with Jaya Bhaduri, *Anamika*. And the whole world knows that in Ramesh Sippy's *Sholay*, Sanjeev played her father-in-law. In A. Bhim Singh's *Naya Din Nayee Raat*, Sanjeev played nine roles opposite Jaya. Yash Chopra's *Trishul* and B.R. Chopra's *Pati Patni Aur Woh* released in May and July 1978 respectively—and the two films were totally different from each other.

In an interview with me, he once said, 'I wanted to be like other actors who played romantic roles and sang songs, running around trees. But working on stage changed my concept and helped me a lot, and I found myself improving. I learnt that an actor has to justify the given character. I got confidence after working on stage. Whenever I watch an English movie, I always think what I can do to make it better. I always watch films from the actor's point of view, trying to find something new in the role. Sometimes I practise particular characters in front of the mirror to improve myself. I advise newcomers to do stage.'

During my association with him, I never saw him lose his temper with any director, journalist, fan or any other person. He didn't bother much about publicity either. In his entire film career, he never kept a personal PRO. His sartorial sense was also in keeping with his down-to-earth lifestyle. No costly, fashionable suits for him. He was a simple person who was most comfortable in a kurta pyjama or in a silk kurta and lungi with simple slippers. I realized that he was shy and introvert. Whenever he was in stress or tense, he smoked a lot. But he never discussed his feelings with anyone. I think that, and his liking for alcohol, took a toll on his health. He used to sit with his friends every evening and drink till late in the night. He had a mind-boggling capacity to hold his drink. That was also one reason he was always late for his film shoots.

But these very friends deserted him in his last days, when he had stopped drinking. Unlike the many rumours and reports that he was a loner who preferred to spend time alone, he loved the company of his friends. He was what one would call *yaaron ka yaar*. Whenever he met his friends, he did so warmly. It broke him when they left him once he'd given up drinking. During the dubbing of *Rahee*, Sanjeev told his director Raman Kumar, 'Nowadays I am alone at home, nobody comes to see me in the evening because I've stopped drinking.' A fortnight before his death, he called his tailor friend Rohidas (Kiran) to his place and said, 'My friends were here only for the drink, they were only friends for a glass of wine.'

Unfortunately, my association with Sanjeev wasn't destined to last long. He passed away less than two and a half years after our first meeting. In this short period, I met him several times but did very few interviews. I observed him a lot. But I never thought that one day I would write a book on him. The credit for that idea goes to Yusuf Sahab (Dilip Kumar). Interestingly, it was Sanjeev's performance in H.S. Rawail's *Sunghursh*, which starred Dilip Kumar, that first caught the attention of film-makers and critics, for the way Sanjeev held his own against the veteran thespian. One evening I was sitting with Yusuf Sahab at his Pali Hill bungalow when he asked me, 'Why can't you do a book on Sanjeev Kumar? He was such a great actor.' That sowed the seeds of this book. It hasn't been easy. For one, Sanjeev Kumar was no longer alive, so I had little first-hand information. But his family helped me a lot. His younger sister, Gayatri Patel, sister-in-law Jyoti Jariwala, Prafulla and nephew Uday Jariwala were available with information at every stage. And then there were Sanjeev's colleagues and friends from the industry, who were more than forthcoming. I realized how much goodwill he had created in his short life.

While I was researching the book and interviewing people from the film industry, God was carving out a different course to make the biography more exclusive and informative. I came across Sumant Batra, who had a great deal of information and exclusive reports on the legendary actor. At my behest, he agreed to collaborate with me as co-author. I am thankful to him, and also to our common friend Shantanu Ray Chaudhuri, who helped us give the book its present shape.

Not a day goes by when I do not think of Sanjeev Kumar and the time we spent together. This book is my humble tribute to a wonderful man. I hope it results in more people coming forward to provide a more comprehensive account of the man, his life and films.

I would also like to thank my wife, Tasmina Zaveri; my son, Tauseef Zaveri; my daughter, Humaira Motiwala; my daughter-in-law, Tanvi Zaveri; and son-in-law, Salman Motiwala, without whose support this book would not have been possible.

Mumbai   Hanif Zaveri
May 2021

Co-author's Note

I had just stepped into my teens when I first watched *Sholay*, which introduced Sanjeev Kumar to me. Neither had I heard of the actor before that, nor did I pay any attention to his performance in the film, its grandeur being too overwhelming for my age and time. It was a few years later, while watching *Naya Din Nayee Raat* on Doordarshan, that I noticed the actor and his extraordinary talent. In what is doubtlessly Sanjeev Kumar's magnum opus, he played nine roles representing the nine rasas, laying out one character after the other—a cigar-chomping wealthy widower; an alcoholic boor who frequents brothels in search of love; an elderly psychiatrist; a fugitive; a fake godman; a rich man turned leper; an effeminate theatre actor; a valiant hunter; and, finally, the lover of the film's heroine—essaying each role deftly. His range left me spellbound. I instantly became an admirer of this great actor.

In the 1970s, like most youngsters of that time, I too was starstruck with Amitabh Bachchan, but it was watching Sanjeev Kumar portray the entire gamut of the human experience that made me appreciate cinema as a form of art. Sanjeev Kumar was in a league of his own, one of cinema's most prolific stars, one if its finest actors.

All he cared about was the integrity of his performance and the intensity of his role.

Tragically, Sanjeev Kumar, who enacted dozens of unforgettable aged characters, did not live to see even fifty summers. He died way too early, at forty-seven. His death was a huge loss for Indian cinema, and for his fans. There was an immense reservoir of his brilliance yet to be tapped. The body of work that he left behind remains a treat to watch, and it's worth mentioning that even over thirty years after his death he remains among the most mimicked actors of all time. His style informs the works of many actors who came after him. Indeed, he remains the gold standard when it comes to the art and craft of acting. He remains an actor's actor in the truest sense of the phrase. Sanjeev Kumar was a complete actor.

When my friend Yasser Usman mentioned that Sanjeev Kumar's family had authorized Hanif Zaveri to author the late actor's biography, I promptly reached out to Hanif Bhai and offered my support for the book. He graciously accepted my enthusiastic offer and I ended up co-writing the book. As a great fan of Sanjeev Kumar, I remain indebted to both Yasser and Hanif Bhai for the opportunity of participating in this work. I must acknowledge that Hanif Bhai did most of the heavy-lifting. I have only attempted to add my two pennies' worth to the hard work he shouldered. He is entitled to receive credit for this book.

I owe a word of thanks to some lovely people at Cinemaazi who contributed to the making of this book. Shantanu Ray Chaudhuri, the consulting editor, deserves a special mention for meticulously editing the book. Nildeep Paul, the project manager, for coordination on all fronts. Priya Basu and Madhubanti De, who reviewed the first draft. Rajeev, who pulled out the material and assets we needed from Cinemaazi's archive.

My gratitude to Shatrughan Sinha-ji for readily agreeing to pen the foreword, and to Bharathi Pradhan for facilitating it.

A special word of gratitude to Milee Ashwarya at Penguin, for her belief in the book, and her team for steering it with thorough professionalism and speed.

This book is not a scholarly essay on the roles Sanjeev Kumar played or his acting prowess. I am no film historian. Nor am I otherwise qualified to decipher his acting or roles as an expert. I am a fan of the actor, a huge fan. My contribution is that of an admirer of his films. There isn't a film of his that I have not watched. The book is a tribute to the late actor's tragically short but impactful life and career—from his childhood years to his foray into cinema, from the initial struggle to his breakthrough, the episodes and tragedies that shaped his life and career, his unfulfilled dreams. In terms of the writing and style, the book is in some way an imitation of Sanjeev Kumar's style of acting—simple, free-flowing and straight from the heart.

We have made all possible efforts to be accurate with facts and avoid mistakes. For any error that might have yet crept in, I take full responsibility.

New Delhi   Sumant Batra
August 2021

1

The Jariwalas

India, in the latter half of the nineteenth century.

Large-scale, machine-based industries were being established, and Indian traders were finally beginning to experience economic prosperity. The Jariwalas, a small but well-respected family in Surat, Gujarat, had been riding the wave of this sudden economic boom. Having invested in the textile industry, they had accumulated a great deal of wealth.

'Jariwala' translates to someone who deals with *zari* (brocade). Shivlal Jagjivan Jariwala, the patriarch of the Jariwala family, had derived his surname from his line of work of getting pure gold zari intricately stitched into exquisite saris. His business had flourished. His carriage, drawn by two magnificent horses, dashed through the busy streets of Surat, leaving awed passers-by in its wake.

Shivlal was devoted to his family and was a doting father to his children, Jethalal and Parvati. Born in 1902, Jethalal was a bright student, but his consuming desire to contribute to their business led him to quit school just after the sixth grade and volunteer to help his father instead. Shivlal took him under his wing and taught him the nitty-gritty of their zari business.

Back in the day, it was common practice to get married early. Jethalal's sister, Parvati, was already married, and Shivlal now proceeded to find a bride for Jethalal. In 1918, at the tender age of sixteen, Jethalal married Shanti, a beautiful girl from the reputed Chakawala family.

Jethalal was blessed with two daughters—Laxmi, born in 1919, and Jaswanti, known as Jassu, born in 1921. However, his happiness was short-lived. Soon after the birth of his second child, he lost his father to a cardiac arrest. Hardly had he begun to recover from his loss when Shanti was diagnosed with tuberculosis—she succumbed to her ailment about a year later.

Mourning the loss of his young bride, yet following the advice of his elders, Jethalal agreed to a second marriage for the sake of his young daughters. It was hard to find a match for him; those who did agree wanted to send both his daughters away to boarding school. Eventually, in March 1923, Jethalal got married for the second time and rechristened his new wife 'Shanti', who bore him his third daughter, Bhagwati, on 25 February 1925.

This marriage, too, was short-lived. Barely ten months after Bhagwati's birth, Shanti died, leaving Jethalal alone to raise his two young daughters and a ten-month-old infant. Unable to manage, Jethalal sent Bhagwati to her maternal uncle, Heeralal Ranchoddas, and concentrated on his business. He partnered with his cousin Naginbhai and expanded his zari business from Surat to Bombay. He established a shop called S. Jagjivan at 2nd Bhoiwada, Bhuleshwar, and invested in two rooms in Tank Building, near the shop, to function as a zari workshop. He started exporting and soon purchased a four-storey building in the prestigious area of Santa Cruz in Bombay. He named his new residence 'Shanti Bhawan', in honour of the women who bore him his much-loved children.

Jethalal was a generous man who never hesitated to extend monetary help to his sister, Parvati. Balkrishna, son of Bhagwati, remembers how Jethalal not only protected his sister's rights of inheritance but also granted her his share.

As Jethalal's business prospered, his well-wishers urged him to marry again.

In a village called Niyode, there lived a fourteen-year-old girl, Javerben, who had recently divorced her mentally unstable husband. Her father, Narain Prabhu Patel, was growing concerned about both his daughters' futures, because one was a divorcee and the other had congenital disabilities. When he found out about Jethalal's search for a third wife, he did not hesitate to offer Javerben's hand, despite the vast age difference. Poverty-stricken and helpless as Narain Prabhu was, this was an opportunity he couldn't let pass. However, local customs dictated that a fine would be levied by the Patel community if the women married outside the village. Unable to afford the hefty fine, Narain Prabhu fell at the feet of the community elders, who took mercy on him and allowed him to give his daughter in marriage to Jethalal.

Jethalal and Javerben tied the knot within a week of meeting each other. The year was 1933. Once again, Jethalal attempted to rename her 'Shanti', but his relatives warned him against it as it had brought him bad luck twice. Reluctantly, Jethalal agreed but stuck to a close variation of the name, Shanta.

Shantaben was only fifteen when she married Jethalal, but she quickly settled into her new life. Kalpana Jariwala, her granddaughter, fondly says:

> Whoever says that a stepmother cannot care for you like your biological mother is wrong. My *nani*, Shantaben, proves them wrong.

Jethalal's eldest daughter, Laxmi, was the same age as her stepmother, and they shared a special bond. When Jethalal decided that it was time for Laxmi to settle down, Shantaben stepped up and performed all the duties of a doting mother, a loving elder sister and a dear friend.

Around this time, Jethalal decided to shift to Bombay from Surat with his entire family and started living in Shanti Bhawan. In 1935,

Shantaben became pregnant with their first child. Sadly, the child, christened Bhawna, caught a cold when she was only three months old and passed away soon after.

In 1937, Laxmi married Vasant Parekh, a young man from their community. Soon after the wedding, Shantaben conceived again. Jethalal was on his way from Santa Cruz to Bhuleshwar when he heard the news, and he stopped at the Mumba Devi Mandir in Pydhonie Zaveri Bazaar to pray for a son. He took exceptional care of Shantaben throughout her pregnancy, and on 9 July 1938, Jethalal and Jassu waited patiently outside the delivery room at Mojesh Hospital, Santa Cruz. At around 2.30 p.m., Shantaben gave birth to a boy. Jethalal named him Harihar, after Lord Krishna, and threw a lavish party in Surat to celebrate his birth.

Soon after, Shantaben found Jassu a perfect groom in Laxmi's brother-in-law, Natwarlal. Harihar was only six months old when the wedding took place, and, in the same year, Jassu was blessed with her first daughter, Ila—Shantaben and Jethalal's first grandchild. Bhagwati was now fourteen years old. Shantaben began to personally train her in household affairs, such as cooking for a big family and caring for an infant. Soon, a proposal arrived for Bhagwati from a reputed Gujarati family. Jethalal approved of the alliance, and wedding celebrations began once more.

On 29 January 1942, Jethalal and Shantaben were blessed with another son, Kishore. Shantaben gave birth to two more children: a girl, Gayatri, on 15 May 1946, and another son called Narayan (or Nikul, as he was popularly known), on 18 May 1948.

While all this was occurring, India became free from the British rule and became an independent nation. Amid the political upheavals of Partition, Jethalal suffered a massive heart attack in November 1949 and passed away at his Santa Cruz residence before anyone had a chance to call the doctor. He was only forty-seven years old. Shantaben was shattered; Harihar was just eleven years old, while Kishore was seven and Gayatri and

Narayan were mere infants, and she had to take care of them all by herself. Harihar, being the eldest, performed his father's last rites, with little idea as to the responsibility that had befallen his young shoulders.

2

Hard Times

No sooner had Jethalal passed away than Shantaben found herself abandoned by everyone, even those she had been certain she could count on. As if tragedy wasn't finished with the family, Jethalal's trusted business partner, Naginbhai, used Shantaben's lack of experience to his benefit and tricked her into signing papers that transferred much of their property, including their shop, to his name.

Shantaben was devastated—she was uneducated, newly widowed and poverty-stricken. But she was also resilient and no stranger to hardships. She decided to fight a legal battle for her rights, and refused any help, even from her father. Meanwhile, far from supporting her endeavours, the Patel community constantly tried to dissuade her on the grounds that the courts were no place for women and that legal battles would drain whatever little wealth they had left.

Surviving as a single mother in a city like Bombay is a humungous challenge even today. Shantaben's family kept urging her to move to Gujarat, but in Gujarat her children would have never received the opportunities which Bombay had to offer. Gayatri Patel recalls:

My mother refused to leave Bombay for the sake of our future.

Finally, Shantaben's family lent their support in other ways. Her mother and brothers would frequently visit her in Bombay to look after the household and the children, so that Shantaben could have some respite to attend to other pressing matters. Finances were dwindling so fast that they had to rent out most of Shanti Bhawan and keep just two rooms for themselves. This did not pay much either—barely Rs 300 monthly—and the family struggled to make ends meet.

In the ongoing legal battle, Shantaben lost her husband's shop but won the rights to the two rooms in Tank Building. She had to surrender ownership of Shanti Bhawan, thereby losing her rental income. However, Shantaben was not one to give up. She launched another legal battle, against not only her disloyal tenants (who had taken advantage of the situation and stopped paying her rent) but also against the Government of India for taking away what was rightfully hers.

Harihar was a sixth-grade student in Sacred Heart Boys High School, Khar, when the family had to shift from their plush Santa Cruz residence to Bhuleshwar. The reputed English-medium school was now far beyond their means. Travelling to school every day as well as paying his fees became increasingly difficult. It broke Shantaben's heart to do it, but she had to take him out of the English-medium school and enrol him in Seth Parmanandas Tribhovandas Vidhyalay, also known as Nanavati Vidhyalay, a Gujarati-medium school located in the same building in which they lived. The school's owner, Thakurdas Gokuldas Nanavati, a lawyer by profession, graciously welcomed Harihar into his school and also shouldered Shantaben's legal troubles.

The school's principal, Chintamani Madhavrao Pandya, who died in 2018, recalled Harihar with fondness:

When Harihar joined our school, I asked all the teachers to take special care of this boy as he had come from an English-medium background to the Gujarati-medium school.

Shantaben enrolled her other children in Nanavati Vidhyalay as well. To meet the costs of living, she had to put one of the two rooms they owned up for rent, at Rs 125 a month, and shift into the remaining room with her children. Gone were the magnificent quarters of Shanti Bhawan. Life at Bhuleshwar was tough, but Shantaben was made of sterner stuff. She gathered all her husband's contacts, deciding to manufacture and sell zari with the help of some old employees. She sold the zari they made to local shops at wholesale rates and exported it overseas. Gayatri Patel remembers:

> My mother would wake up early in the morning, cook for us and leave for work, returning only at night.

Given their circumstances, Hari felt guilty about accepting even the meagre pocket money his mother gave him. His conscience urged him to be of greater help to her. Since Shantaben would never allow him to compromise on his studies, Hari took it upon himself to help with her work in the evenings. He would diligently wrap zaris into neat parcels, carefully write down the recipients' addresses on the packages and walk to two post offices with the heavy bundles balanced on his young shoulders, to wait in serpentine queues. No matter how hard he toiled, he never felt satisfied.

One day, Hari found his mother in tears, distraught that a valued customer had returned her package, and declared that he would not continue business with her. The young boy declared:

> Baa, I have decided to find a job for myself. I can't see you like this, struggling and supporting the family alone.

Shantaben was alarmed and forbade him from giving up his studies, lovingly placating him with the assurance that everything would be better in a few years. Hari reluctantly gave in and shelved the idea of taking up a job. Shantaben's well-meaning promise was difficult to achieve. The family of four lived and worked out of a single room. For Hari, concentrating on his studies with so many distractions was difficult. His class teacher, Chotubhai Heeralal Intwala, came to his rescue:

> In our school, there was a study room for students, which I offered to Hari. After school, Hari would sit there and finish his homework.

Hari and Intwala shared a mutual love for theatre and dramatics, an interest that nurtured their friendship. Intwala was a maths and science teacher who also taught dramatics. Two periods each week were devoted to writing short plays on an allotted subject, and the ones selected were performed before the teachers and students. According to C.M. Pandya:

> I remember Harihar's performance, but I never thought that this young boy would become a big superstar and earn so much popularity in Hindi cinema!

Plays were usually written and performed in Gujarati, but Hari wrote and performed in Hindi. The only problem, C.H. Intwala remembers, was that he never wrote a role for a female character, although theirs was a co-educational school.

Hari took an interest in sports as well, playing both table tennis and cricket remarkably well. Nanavati Vidhyalay organized inter-school cricket matches at Oval Ground, Churchgate, where Hari played as a batsman. During one of these tournaments, he made friends with a bowler from a competing school who, just like him, loved everything to do with cricket and movies. Fortunately, his new friend lived nearby and they met frequently. Years later, the two friends would make a huge mark in the film industry—one would be immortalized on screen as Sanjeev Kumar, while the other would become the well-known character actor Satyen Kappu.

Ramesh Babubhai Patel, then captain of Moti Sheri Cricket Club, recalls:

During the summer vacations, he would come to Surat by express train and head straight to my house, to request me to arrange cricket matches for a week. We would arrange at least ten matches at Suleman Ground, near Surat Station, which has now been converted into a bus depot . . .

Chandrakanth Chatiyawala, the then vice-captain, says:

Hari was not in our cricket team, but we took him as a guest player.

Members of the Moti Sheri Cricket Club contributed Rs 3 each for cricket gear, but they never took any contribution from their beloved Hari. In Surat, Hari spent most of his time with his close friends, but he also made it a point to visit his stepsister and maternal uncles at Niyode. Good-natured and amiable, he made friends wherever he went. Harshad and Anil Desai became Hari's close friends. Harshad Desai remembers how Hari learnt to play the harmonium from his father. Anil Desai reminisces:

We used to sit with him in our *wada* [courtyard] until midnight. Our dinner consisted of jawar roti with vegetables, pickles and papad.

On one occasion, they organized a picnic at the famous Dumas Beach, which was at a distance of 10 km from Surat. This outing was memorable because Hari performed a small skit for his friends at the beach. According to Ramesh Babubhai Patel:

Yes! He wore a sari and performed in front of us—we will never forget that!

The Hari in Bombay was quite different from the one in Surat. In Surat, he was carefree and didn't think twice before announcing his passion for theatre to his friends. In Bombay, he kept his love for the stage a secret, as his desire would clash with the dreams his mother had for his future.

Shantaben began having second thoughts about Hari continuing in Nanavati Vidhyalay. She realized that the Gujarati-medium school could not offer the opportunities that an English-medium school could. How could he become a doctor or a lawyer if he didn't know English well? While she was considering shifting Hari to another school, it was becoming evident that her son's interests had already moved away from academics.

Hari had just watched *Baiju Bawra* (1952) with his friend Naderbhai, and he could not stop talking about it or stop thinking about Meena Kumari. He had never spoken about his love for movies to his mother, but she noticed how enthralled he was with the prospect of acting, and this seriously alarmed her. She visited C.H. Intwala, hoping that he would guide Hari in the right direction, only to discover that the teacher was the culprit. In the following weeks, she observed how Hari became increasingly drawn towards the world of cinema. He walked a great distance just to take a look at the film posters outside cinemas. Shantaben could no longer ignore it. Her dreams of making Hari the doctor or lawyer he was destined to become were rapidly slipping away from her. She once again spoke to the teacher whom she held responsible for kindling this desire for theatre in the young and highly impressionable Hari's heart. She confronted him:

Teachers build their students' careers and you are spoiling my son's prospects! I am sending my son to your school to help him seek an education and you are encouraging him to take up acting? What will he become? Is he Prithviraj Kapoor's son? Who will give him a chance to act? Sir, we are poor people, we cannot dream as big as Harihar is dreaming.

Hari's teacher heard her out patiently and then replied:

Madam, is your son not serious in his studies? Does he not attend his classes regularly? He is one of the best students in the school. Every teacher loves him, including the principal. Your son is on the right path to success. He is a good student and also happens to be a wonderful actor. Being a dramatics teacher, I am just doing my job by encouraging him.

Years later, in 1981, C.H. Intwala approached Hari to be the chief guest for Nanavati Vidhyalaya's annual Sharad Utsav. By then, Hari was a star. Not only did he graciously accept his teacher's request, but he also delivered a speech at the festival, honouring his mentor's contribution to his career.

3

Hansuya

Shantaben had braved legal battles, fought seasoned tradesmen and had courageously rebuilt their family business, but when it came to her eldest son, she couldn't help but feel disconcerted. She had envisioned Hari as a renowned doctor who would heal hundreds of patients with his magical touch, or as a celebrated lawyer who would move the jury with his sheer eloquence—in short, a man of letters and a respectable member of society. Hari was her investment to a better future, her strength to face a fresh battle every day, the one for whom she had sacrificed all her comforts because he, Shantaben believed, was no ordinary child; he would redeem them from their life of misery and be the son his father had always wished for.

The boy who was supposed to rise to such honourable heights had declared that his life's ambition was to become an actor. Shantaben knew how nepotism, affluence and destiny played a crucial part in a budding actor's career. She was certain that Hari was headed for disaster and saw only one way to get him back to his senses: she conspired with Bhagwati to get the errant Hari married. Domesticating Hari, according to his mother and sister, seemed the only way to make him realize his erroneous ways and get over his delusions. All he needed was a home-loving wife. It didn't matter that he was sixteen.

Mother and daughter set forth on their secret mission seeking prospective brides. Bhagwati zeroed in on Hansuya, also known as Hansa, a Gujarati girl who lived in the neighbourhood. Hansuya had an agreeable disposition, came from a well-to-do and respectable family, and her elder sister, Padma, was already married (an essential marital criterion at the time). Her brother-in-law, Champaklal, happened to be a friend of Hari's. Shantaben was certain that this was a match made in heaven. A marriage proposal was sent to Hansuya, and her parents accepted it whole-heartedly. Hari didn't have a clue about what was transpiring.

One fine day, Shantaben called Hari to her and told him that he was to be engaged the next day. Hari was dumbstruck. A simple *shagun* ceremony was held, and, before Hari could even register what was happening, Hansuya and he were engaged to be married.

Hari's silence was mistaken for compliance. Gradually, he made it amply clear that he didn't like Hansuya and did not believe her to be a good match for him. Shantaben, however, was a woman of her word, and she had promised Hansuya's father, Madanlal Khushaldas, that she would treat Hansuya like her own daughter. As Hansuya recalls:

> Whenever Baa came to Surat, she invited me to stay with her for a week and I spent some quality time with her at Moti Sheri. Even during my vacations, I stayed with her family at Tank Building, Bhuleshwar. She took me to Harihar's mama's (maternal uncle) house at Niyode, where we stayed with her entire family.

Although Hari ignored his fiancé, the rest of his family lavished their attention on her. Her arrival was always associated with fun and laughter as Hari's siblings and their friends would all gather together to play cards and chat for hours. Gayatri was only eight years old, but she remembers that her brother never took any interest in Hansuya.

Most times he would not even be home when she came over. During 1954–7, Hansuya visited the Jariwalas on several occasions, but Hari never warmed to her. Hansuya says:

> It made me feel very bad. Back then I couldn't share my feelings with anyone. At one point, I realized that he disliked me because I was not good-looking or educated enough for him. He knew he deserved someone better.

Engagements usually culminated in marriage within months. Hari and Hansuya's engagement lasted years because Hari was reluctant to tie the knot and Shantaben couldn't bring herself to tell Hansuya's parents. This bothered Hari.

One day, when Shantaben resumed her talks about Hari's wedding, he interrupted her:

> Baa, I'm a hundred per cent certain that I am not going to marry her. Convey this to her parents, otherwise, she will grow old waiting for me and it will be difficult for her parents to find a suitable match for her.

And that was the end of the engagement. Both families parted ways with heavy hearts.

Years later, Hari and Hansuya bumped into each other at a wedding ceremony in Baroda. He was with his mother and she was on her own. Her first marriage with Hasmukh Bhai was in trouble, and she was struggling financially. When Shantaben learnt of her troubles, she spoke to Hari about helping the girl whom she had vowed to treat as a daughter. Hari had already undergone a celluloid metamorphosis and was known to the world as Sanjeev Kumar. Perhaps he also nurtured some guilt about having rejected Hansuya all those years ago. He stepped up to help Hansuya.

Hansuya clarifies that she has no regrets about not marrying Sanjeev Kumar:

He was not in my destiny. And to me, he was Harihar, not Sanjeev Kumar. His film *Aandhi* is my favourite film—I saw it over twenty times! I like his *Raja Aur Runk* and *Sholay* also. My second husband, Dhanji, was his fan and always wanted to meet him. In 1983, when we came to Bombay, I took him to Harihar's friend's bungalow in Juhu where I knew he was staying. But his secretary, Jamnadas, didn't allow us to meet him. My husband and I saw him from a distance, sitting on a chair and reading a newspaper. This memory will remain etched in my mind till the end of my life.

Her husband adds,

On that fateful day in 1985, I was in the market buying groceries when someone told me that Sanjeev Kumar had passed away. I immediately bought a Gujarati newspaper in which Harihar's photograph was printed along with the news of his demise. When I showed it to Hansuya, she could not stop crying. That day she only prayed for him, without eating a morsel of food or drinking a drop of water.

4

Foray into Acting

Hari knew his destiny was irrevocably tied to Indian cinema, but many hurdles stood between him and his goal. Overcoming most of them required divine intervention, but some, like his voice, he believed he could work on.

'Yes, he was worried about his weak voice,' affirms C.H. Intwala. Hari worked hard on his dialogue delivery, practising the same lines in various pitches and tones and modulating them with different hues of emotional intensity. His guide C.H. Intwala would supervise his dialogue-reading sessions every evening. At the time, Hari had no idea that the voice he was striving to alter would one day help him carve a niche for himself in the world of cinema, and, later, would become a staple for mimicry artists, although they would find it near impossible to reproduce the various nuances that affected his tone.

Hari deduced that if he wished to take his career forward, he would have to be trained professionally. Producer Sashadhar Mukherjee's acting school, Filmalaya, had a good reputation.

Hari rushed to gain admission, but, to his disappointment, learnt that the fee was way beyond his reach.

The walk back home wasn't easy that day. He wondered if his family would have been so impoverished had his father been alive. His mother was nothing less than a warrior, but there were times when he sorely needed a father figure, and this was one such day. Distressed, he entered the house after ten at night and went straight to bed. His mother, sensing that something was wrong, went to talk to him. Hari was overwhelmed with despair and words failed him; his innocent face was clouded with sorrow, he seemed to have aged beyond his years. Shantaben ran her fingers through his dark curls and comforted her son. Her kindness troubled him further, and he felt guilty and ashamed of his unreasonable demands. Reprimanding himself, he tried to tell her that he needed money but hesitated, then broke down and told her. Shantaben held up her hand, indicating that he must say no more. She would sell her jewellery to finance his admission—as a widow, she was forbidden from wearing coloured clothes or ornaments anyway.

Hari refused, firmly standing his ground, and mother and son argued into the wee hours. They finally decided to pawn her jewellery. As soon as Hari had found his footing, he would buy it back. Shantaben coerced him into action the very next morning, ensuring that he paid the full fees and began his classes.

In an interview with Ameen Sayani, recorded in 1974, Sanjeev Kumar spoke at length about the relationship he shared with his mother:

> She is my closest friend, someone who knows all my moods, my likes and dislikes. She helps me solve my problems. When I'm hurt or upset, I cry on her lap, and she puts her hand on my head and gives me the courage to stand up and fight my destiny; she is the one who helps me keep my patience. She has one complaint against me though, that I don't visit the temple enough. I tell her that I don't believe in God, I can't believe in someone I cannot see. I believe in you. You are my mother, my friend and my God.

So did he manage to retrieve his mother's gold from the pawnbroker? You bet he did!

P.D. Shenoy taught acting at Filmalaya. Many of his students went on to become successful actors, including Sadhana, Asha Parekh and Joy Mukherjee. Shenoy had a unique method of teaching. He would assign a character complete with a backstory to each of his students and ask them to give an impromptu performance based on the guidelines. Hari was a natural, flitting in and out of complex characters in the blink of an eye. Mohan Makijany, better known as Mac Mohan, was Hari's batchmate. He is best remembered for playing Samba in *Sholay* (1975), in which Hari played Thakur. Who knew back then that two students from the same batch would become part of one of Hindi cinema's most seminal works of art?

Behroz, a Parsi teacher, helped the students with their voice modulation and diction. Under her training, Hari worked on modulating his voice, but it was still far from the heavy baritone expected of actors. His voice tended to sound high-pitched whenever he raised it. However, this never affected the quality of his acting. When he famously said, '*Gabbar, yeh haath nahin phaansi ka phanda hai,*' in *Sholay*, his voice added an evocative layer of tragedy to the formidable Thakur. Years later, Behroz fell in love with make-up artist Sarosh Modi and married him. Sarosh became the personal make-up man to Hari.

One day, actor Mahesh Desai came to Filmalaya to meet Behroz. While he waited for her, he watched the students perform a short, one-act play called *Marriages Arranged*, and saw Hari in action for the first time. With no introduction, Mahesh Desai immediately spotted the potential of the young actor.

Filmalaya's founder, Sashadhar Mukherjee, realized it was time for Hari to move on to a bigger platform. He spoke to him personally and advised him to join the Indian People's Theatre Association (IPTA). Humble and respectful, Hari always paid heed to his advice and rushed to IPTA to attain membership. There he met A.K. Hangal, who, speaking to me, remembered him as a dishevelled young man,

. . . wearing a creased white kurta pyjama and a pair of slippers which had seen better days . . .

To him, Hari seemed talented but lacked the personality of an actor.

I thought to myself, 'How can he become an actor?'

Unable to dash his hopes, Hangal told him he would let him know if any roles came up for him.

In a month, Hangal began casting for *Damru*, a new play he planned to direct. Although Hari trudged to his door every day to remind him of his promise, Hangal cast Sudhir Dalvi instead. Dalvi was an architect who was slated to design the set but took up the role at Hangal's insistence. Although Hari was not cast in *Damru*, he turned up for the rehearsals every day, quietly sitting in a corner and watching the actors perform.

One day, Director R.M. Singh noticed Hari. Singh was working on a short street play, *Majma*, and offered Hari the role of a magician who sold amulets and talismans on the streets. Hari accepted gratefully and *Majma* was ready to hit the streets after just four days of rehearsals, despite Hari's sixty-page-long dialogues. When Hangal saw Hari perform, he realized that he had underestimated the boy. He was astonished to see that many in the crowd did not even realize that he was performing and thought he was actually selling amulets! Hangal now rushed to cast Hari in *Damru*. As there were no other roles left, the nineteen-year-old Hari was cast as the sixty-year-old father of six children.

Hari would go on to play an old man in many plays, earning the nickname '*Juni Jari*' (Old Jari). Many years later, actress Tabassum asked Sanjeev Kumar why he kept accepting roles where he'd have to play the part of an old man. He replied that a fortune-teller had predicted that he wouldn't live long enough to grow old and so, he was trying to live out an age that would never come his way in real life.

Shaukat Kaifi recalls being shocked when 'Hangal Sahab' cast her opposite Hari in the play. When she learnt that he was only nineteen years old, she wondered how this young boy would play a bank manager. She asked Hangal,

Do you want to make a flop play? This is a very difficult role and you are risking it by giving it to this young boy!

Hangal, however, was confident of Hari's abilities. Shaukat Kaifi agreed to play his wife, a woman who had lost her sanity due to financial crises. She fondly remembered:

Hari got a huge round of applause from the audience, the loudest one ever, and I was ignored and forgotten. He had got his make-up done in such a way that, at first, even I could not recognize him backstage. He worked extremely hard on his sixty-year-old character, internalizing it so well that sitting, standing, talking and walking, he would look like a sixty-year-old bank manager. His dialogues were popular amongst the audience, 'Mehnat karo bhai mehnat—tabhi aap aage badhoge, tabhi tarakki hogi, aadmi ban jaaoge aadmi.'

She could not have imagined then that, years later, the same boy would play her daughter Shabana's hero in the film *Vishwasghaat* (1977). By then, he had become Sanjeev Kumar. To Shaukat Kaifi, he always remained Harihar. She once introduced him as Sanjeev Kumar to her friends and he rebuked her affectionately:

When did I become Sanjeev Kumar to you?

R.M. Singh and A.K. Hangal were both impressed by Hari's performance. Working with him was easy because he didn't need much time to understand the requirements of his role and slipped into character and improvised in scenes easily. He was of an amiable, humorous disposition, qualities that were instrumental in dissipating tensions bound to build up in stressful environments. In a short period, he became famous at IPTA, and notable directors like Balraj Sahani, Kaifi Azmi, Prem Dhawan, K.A. Abbas, Salil Chaudhary, Sulbha Arya, Ramesh Talwar, Basu Bhattacharya and Vishwamitter Adil were all praises.

Nevertheless, there remained one colossal problem in Hari's life: money. He would take stringent measures to save every paisa he could, often travelling great distances on foot. His friends, Satyen Kappu and Sudhir Dalvi, would walk with him from Warden Road to Bhuleshwar. However, like most young people, he often spent the money he so carefully saved on trivialities. Sudhir Dalvi recounts:

> One day, while returning from our rehearsals at Kemps Corner, a boy selling flowers called out to Hari, 'Hero, *ye phool le na!*'

Delighted to be addressed as 'hero', he bought the flowers immediately.

Sudhir Dalvi remembers another incident that became almost prophetic for Hari. When Dharmendra's first film, *Dil Bhi Tera Hum Bhi Tere* (1960), hit the theatres, Hari, Dalvi and Satyen Kappu went to watch it. Seeing Dharmendra on screen, Hari complained:

> Producers are insane. They will cast a bodybuilder as a hero but will not give a chance to a person like me. What does this boy have except his physique?

Sudhir Dalvi assured him:

> Your time will come and you will get your chance to act with him.

And so he did, in two blockbuster movies, *Seeta Aur Geeta* (1972) and *Sholay.*

Meanwhile, writer–director Sagar Sarhadi's play *Main Aaghuta Hoon* was in a crisis. Four days before the opening, the actor playing the lead role was hospitalized—indefinitely. Eager to release the play on time, Sarhadi decided to get in touch with Hari for the main role upon R.M. Singh's suggestion and, together with R.M. Singh, he paid a visit to Hari at his Bhuleshwar residence. Although Hari was taken aback to see his unannounced guests, as soon as he learnt of the situation, he agreed to take the role. Sagar Sarhadi claims that Hari worked day and night on the script. Within four days, Hari was ready to act his part and they had a successful opening.

Post the rehearsals for *Main Aaghuta Hoon*, the crew decided to head to a bar. Money was being collected from everyone. Sagar Sarhadi recollects:

> When I asked Hari for his contribution, he said he didn't have any money, and I reprimanded him, 'Go home, drink milk and go to sleep.'

Years later, when they were working together again in *Sawaal* (1982) and the crew was heading out for drinks, Sarhadi had no cash on him. Hari repeated what Sarhadi had said to him, then laughed and asked him to join them anyway.

Directors at IPTA had begun to show confidence in Hari. R.M. Singh cast Hari and A.K. Hangal in his new play *Ward No. 6* as Dr Ghosh and Dr Beg respectively. Director Ramesh Talwar says:

> After watching him in *Ward No. 6*, I said to myself, 'What a range this actor has!'

Comedian Javed Khan recalls him as his senior in IPTA, ruing that he had never had the chance to act with Hari on stage.

Hari and Hangal's friendship thrived on their mutual love for the stage and cinema. At times, Hangal became the father figure

Hari sought. At other times, he was the friend from whom Hari could borrow cigarettes. According to A.K. Hangal:

> Those days I bought 50-paisa cigarette boxes with twenty cigarettes in them. Whenever Hari asked me for a cigarette, I would look around to see if anyone was looking, before giving him one . . .

On the sets of *Anamika* (1973), when Hangal asked Hari for a cigarette, Hari imitated Hangal's actions, leaving the veteran actor in splits.

Hari's excellent memory meant that he could learn lengthy dialogues in one or two readings. His mind was sharp, and he could recall perfectly not only his own lines but also his co- actors'. Hangal, however, had difficulty remembering his lines at times.

One day, R.M. Singh had cast Hangal with Hari in a new play called *Imandaar*. Hari was standing in the wings when Hangal was on stage for a particular scene and, much to his dismay, he realized that Hangal had forgotten his lines. Hari did his utmost to prompt Hangal but couldn't do it properly because of the distance. The audience began to boo Hangal. Humiliated, he left the stage and lost his temper at Hari. The situation worsened when a flustered Hangal forgot from which side he had to exit the stage and mistakenly re-entered the stage from the other side.

Despite these minor rubs, Hari remained close to Hangal throughout his career. As Hangal said:

> When we were shooting for *Anamika* he gave an excellent shot without a single retake. Everyone applauded him. I was so involved in the scene that I forgot to clap. The next day I appreciated his performance in his green room, little realizing that he had noticed I didn't clap. He responded by complaining, 'Everyone applauded my performance yesterday, but you didn't.'

Hangal's appreciation often became the paternal approval Hari craved.

At IPTA, artists were not paid because it was an amateur theatre for experimental arts. Hari couldn't go on working with little or no remuneration, so he decided to look beyond IPTA. This was his opportunity to explore other theatres in the city, so he became a part of Gujarati theatre, as a freelance actor. After his first Gujarati play *Chhuta Chheda*'s success with Chandravadhan Bhatt, he was flooded with offers from other groups, such as the Indian National Theatre.

Hindi plays made by reputed directors also came his way, like Manvinder Chitnis's rendition of Arthur Miller's *All My Sons,* called *Do Jahan Ke Beech*. In both Chitnis's and Alyque Padamsee's adaptation of Miller's play (*Sara Sansar Apna Parivar*), Hari once again played an old man to perfection. He was so thorough with the subtle nuances of this character that he became Pravin Joshi's first choice when he decided to adapt *All My Sons* in Gujarati as *Koi No Ladak Vayo* for the Indian National Theatre. Hari carried the distinction of being the only actor in all of Bombay to perform the same role in three different groups. One unfortunate day, while performing *Koi No Ladak Vayo* in Ahmedabad, Hari's dhoti came undone. However, without missing a beat, he calmly gathered up his dhoti and carried on with his dialogues, and no one from the audience even realized the faux pas.

Male actors were paid Rs 35 and female actors Rs 25 for a single show of *Koi No Ladak Vayo*, but Hari asked Pravin Joshi to pay him Rs 50 per show as he had no other source of income. Looking at his financial condition and considering his immense talent, Joshi agreed.

Hari invited his erstwhile teacher C.H. Intwala to watch his Gujarati plays, and Intwala was overjoyed:

I had a feeling that this was just the beginning for Hari. Soon he was going to shine on the silver screen.

Tarla Joshi joined Hari's ever-widening circle of friends during the rehearsals for *Koi No Ladak Vayo* at Jaihind College. It was a friendship that would last his entire lifetime. She became a part of his family, liked by everyone at Bhuleshwar. To Shantaben, she was like a daughter, and to his siblings, she was their very own 'Nani Baa'.

Hari's friends Pravin Joshi, Tarla Joshi, Arvind Joshi and Tarla Mehta, a close bunch, often arranged picnics, driving to Lonavala or Khandala in Mahesh Desai's car, with Hari singing Mukesh's songs all the way. Tarla Mehta recalls how Pravin Joshi and Tarla Joshi often rebuked Hari and her for not taking care of their appearance. Hari's hair, in particular, was always untidy, and his clothes unironed. Fed up with his nonchalance, one day Pravin and Arvind took him to Morning Star salon in Walkeshwar, Malabar Hill, for a haircut, where Hari met Moin Bhai, his hairdresser.

Hari often enjoyed a cup of tea and fluffy Khari biscuits at Allahabeli Restaurant, Forjett, with Sudhir Dalvi and Satyen Kappu, when he rehearsed at Bhulabhai Memorial Institute; he sipped hot coffee at Gaylord Churchgate with Pravin Joshi, Mahesh Desai and Girish Vaidya when he went for INT rehearsals at Jaihind College and had a late-night tipple at C.P. Tank with friends. Those days, the state of Maharashtra was under liquor prohibition. A cool-drink shop at C.P. Tank, owned by a Parsi gentleman called Homi Seth, sold alcohol surreptitiously from 10 p.m. to 2 a.m., and all the theatre artistes would throng to his shop for a nightcap. P.D. Shenoy was also one of them.

Bachu Sampat, one of the INT producers, who never drank at Homi Seth's establishment, visited the place to meet the artists. Homi announced a free round of drinks whenever Bachu Sampat visited his shop, and so Hari tried to pull him along in the hope of a free drink. However, one day the police raided Homi Seth's shop and both Bachu Sampat and Hari were arrested for breaking the prohibition. Luckily, Homi had connections, and both Sampat and Hari were released without much of a scene.

Hari would enjoy a couple of drinks every night after finishing his shows and rehearsals, but this never came in the way of his commitment to theatre. His performance in the play *Jawabi Hamla* by Vishwamitter Adil was remarkable; he played a middle-aged manager and heart-wrenchingly uttered, '*Agar isi tarah aap log karte rahoge toh mere chhote chhote kamsin masoom bachchon ka kya hoga?*'

A struggling artist reached out to Hari after seeing him with Chandravadhan Bhatt, a well-known figure of the Gujarati stage. He couldn't muster the courage to approach Bhatt directly for work, so he asked Hari to put in a word for him. One day, while planning an outdoor show for the play *Niyay Na Panth*, Bhatt discovered that he was one comedian short. Hari used this opportunity to introduce the artist and assured Bhatt that he would do well given a chance. This actor was Dinesh Hingoo, who later went on to become a well-known comedian.

Hari's performance in *Niyay Na Panth* was phenomenal. Birla Sabha Graha, where the play was being performed, was packed to the rafters. Sohrab Modi, one of the most highly acclaimed theatre artists of that era, was performing alongside Hari. Co-artist Sulbha Arya from IPTA remembers that Hari never allowed the fame and popularity of his co-stars to affect his acting. During one performance, he was so deeply immersed in a character that he didn't care who was starring opposite him, a habit that held him in good stead when he started working in Hindi films. In a particular scene with both Hari and Sohrab, the audience was so moved by Hari's dialogues that they applauded him for two whole minutes, making Sohrab wait. Within this mesmerized audience was Jamnadas. Like everyone else, he was completely enraptured by Hari's spellbinding performance. He knew a little about the world of theatre because he had worked for Maganlal Dresswala, supplying costumes to various theatre artists. He had met enough performers to know that Hari was poised on the cusp of greatness. Jamnadas waited patiently to have a word with him backstage. When they finally met and spoke, Jamnadas was enthralled by Hari's unassuming personality.

Jamnadas saw something in Hari that no one else could. At a time when Hari barely made enough money to cover his travel expenses within the city, Jamnadas pledged his allegiance to him and offered his services as Hari's secretary, despite there being no hope

of remuneration on the horizon. Hari was perhaps the only actor
in Bollywood who had a secretary before he had movie contracts.
Jamnadas quizzed the startled Hari,

> Did I ask for a salary? Pay me when you make enough money. I'll
> be with you when you make lots of it. And I'm here now while
> you're struggling to reach there.

Such loyalty was unheard of to Hari, and the incredible confidence
in his talent was deeply motivating. Hari had found another soul
who was laying odds on his future, a person who looked forward to
his success and whose own life and happiness now depended on it.
How could he let him down? Failure was no longer an option. The
only question was, how big could he dream? And how far would he
go to attain his heart's desire?

5

Valuable Lessons

Hari was off to a good start, but he still had a long way to go. In a bid to meet prospective directors and producers, he would walk long distances—from Chembur Railway Station to RK Studio, from Bhuleshwar to Famous Studio, Mahalaxmi, from Andheri Railway Station to Mohan Studio; he walked and walked and kept walking. He wasn't alone on his journey. Jamnadas often accompanied him, and at times even went alone on his behalf.

Funds were perpetually short. Hari scrimped, saved and cut corners wherever he could. He stopped buying cigarettes and would borrow his friends' telephones to make phone calls. He maintained a list of producers and directors and made it a point to visit them in person to ask for work. Meeting them wasn't easy; travelling required money and the efforts often came to naught.

Even though Shantaben supported Hari with the occasional buck, there would still never be enough for clothes. His only clothes were two pairs of white kurta pyjamas, which he had to wash every night so that there would be a fresh set on the next day. 'Heroes' don't dress like that . . . but Hari did.

Filmalaya Production House chose promising students from Filmalaya Acting School and offered them small roles in their films.

On one such occasion, Ram Mukherjee sent his assistant to find him a student actor for his movie *Hum Hindustani* (1960), starring Sunil Dutt and Asha Parekh. The role was small, but the actor would be paid. Upon being approached, Hari immediately accepted the offer of playing a police inspector for Rs 12 per shift. Hari's role had no dialogues, but he gave it his hundred per cent; this was the first time he was facing the camera after all!

Rs 12 per shift was a good sum of money for Hari. He was proud of what he had earned and was elated at handing over his hard-earned money to his mother. Her approval mattered the most to him. Delighted, Shantaben took Hari to Mumba Devi's temple at Zaveri Bazaar and donated a part of his earnings to the temple's fund. When Hari took his mother to watch the movie, and the screen filled up with a shot of his face in close-up, he couldn't help but point to his mother and childishly exclaim, '*Baa, jo main chun* (Mother, that's me)!' Barely catching a glimpse of her son, Shantaben asked him if she would see him on the screen again. Hari laughed as he assured her that she would if she came and watched the movie again.

Seeing Hari as euphoric as this filled Shantaben's heart with joy. She had waited for this day for a very long time. She had promised herself that she would give her son what his father couldn't, the freedom and support he required to succeed, and she was proud of herself as well as her son that day.

Hari wasn't satisfied with just a blink-and-miss, two-second close-up in a movie. He was gifted and his vision was to be a part of well-made films where his talent could shine. Attaining such exalted goals would not be easy. It was an industry steeped in nepotism, and he was a rank outsider with no money to spare for even a new set of clothes.

Hari travelled back and forth, trying to meet directors, producers or their assistants. He journeyed great distances without giving the scorching heat or the infamous Bombay rain much thought, but usually met with disappointment and humiliation.

'*Abhi kaam nahin hai; kuchh hoga toh batayenge* (there is no work
for you at the moment; we'll let you know if something comes up).'
'*Apna* photograph *chhodke jao* (leave your photograph with us).'
'*Baad mein aakar milna; sahab abhi busy hain* (come later; sir is
busy right now).'

Sometimes a glimmer of hope shone for a split second before plunging
him back into darkness. Chandulal Shah, founder of Ranjit Studio
and a well-known film-maker, was looking for actors to cast in his
film *Akeli Mat Jaiyo* (1963). He met Hari and showed an interest in
him, asking him for his photographs. Hari was sure that this was the
big break he had been waiting for and gave Chandulal Shah three
copies of his photographs, each with his name and address at the
back. When he didn't receive any news from Shah the following day,
he decided to visit the studio. Just before he stepped into Shah's
office, Hari's glance fell on the dustbin placed outside the door. His
photographs were lying in the day's garbage. He had never felt so
humiliated before. He turned around and left, vowing never to work
with Shah.

     Actress Dina Pathak was about to direct a Gujarati play called
Vijaya and had a good role chalked out for Hari. Before they could
meet and discuss the play, Hari decided to speak to Tarachand
Barjatya, the founder of Rajshri Productions, since word was out that
they were looking for people to cast in their first film *Aarti* (1962).
The director, Phani Majumdar, had already cast Ashok Kumar and
Meena Kumari, but the male lead had not been finalized. According
to the script, the male protagonist was to be a kurta pyjama-clad,
poverty-stricken young man. When Hari entered Barjatya's office,
Phani Majumdar was also present. Barjatya couldn't picture Hari
as a hero. His dishevelled appearance was enough to guarantee his
rejection. Phani Majumdar, however, could look beyond the facade
of his unkemptness. There was a certain earnestness in Hari's face, a
compelling sense of honesty, that made Majumdar feel he could do
justice to the character. He interrupted their conversation, asking

Hari to come for a screen test. Soon, Majumdar talked Barjatya into casting Hari as the male lead and Hari was overjoyed. This would be his dream film. Not only was it being made by some of the biggest names in the industry, but he was also to be seen opposite Meena Kumari, his favourite Bollywood actress.

Hari was about to embark on a new chapter. Keeping his new commitments in mind, he approached Dina Pathak and politely told her that he would be unable to accept her offer. Dina Pathak was not one to hold grudges and gave him her blessings. Mahesh Desai was present when this occurred, and he recalls seeing Hari in a buoyant mood. Hari's role in the play would eventually be essayed by Prashant Desai.

Perhaps Hari ought to have waited before turning down Dina Pathak's offer. Perhaps he should have checked to ensure that Barjatya was convinced enough to let him play the male lead in his film. Perhaps he would have been less hurt if he hadn't aimed so high. But Hari did not rely on possibilities. He took every chance that came his way to rise above his circumstances.

Very soon he was informed that he was being replaced by an actor called Pradeep Kumar. The reason for his dismissal seemed ludicrous. He was told that his teeth were in bad shape. No one could believe this absurd explanation, and many came up with their own theories. Some said it was Meena Kumari who had persuaded Majumdar to cast Pradeep Kumar opposite her. Others blamed Barjatya's reluctance to cast a newcomer in his first film as a producer.

Hari's confidence was shaken by this incident. He went home late, refused dinner and burrowed beneath his blankets in despair. Shantaben was beside him yet again, speaking words of consolation and encouragement. Her presence gave him the strength to carry on. According to Gayatri Patel:

That moral support was important for Bhai. I don't think that my brother would succeed without my mother's support.

Years later, when Hari had become the successful actor Sanjeev Kumar, the very same Rajshri Production planned a film, *Saaransh* (1984), keeping him in mind, but this time he turned them down. As actress Rohini Hattangadi remembers, she was supposed to feature opposite Sanjeev Kumar in *Saaransh*, but something went wrong between the actor and the production house. She considers herself unfortunate for having missed the opportunity to star opposite Sanjeev Kumar twice, once in *Saaransh* and later in one of Kumar Gaurav's films.

Not everyone treated Hari with such little confidence, though. Director Govind Saraiya, mesmerized by the strength of his performance in a Gujarati play, went backstage and told him that he wanted to introduce him in his film *Saraswatichandra* (1968). Hari was happy to receive this offer, and he readily agreed. Saraiya assured him that the film would only be made with him on board.

Unfortunately, the making of *Saraswatichandra* was delayed. Hari waited for it desperately, but his finances were running low. He was forced to accept the stunt film offers that came his way. Eventually, *Saraswatichandra* was cleared for shooting, but Hari was informed that the director had replaced both the actor and the actress; Hari's role was to be played by Manish and Nimmi's role by Nutan. Hari was deeply disappointed and stormed into Saraiya's office to ask him why he gave the role away. Saraiya explained with regret that appearing in stunt films ruins an actor's image and that he couldn't possibly cast a stunt actor in *Saraswatichandra*.

This proved to be an important lesson for Hari. He learnt that he could not do just any work that came his way—he had to build upon and safeguard his image in the industry. He also realized that he couldn't count on promises. Words were not enough to seal any deal.

Both these incidents, related to Barjatya's *Aarti* and Saraiya's *Saraswatichandra*, left Hari scarred. After the *Aarti* fiasco, his friends often mockingly heralded his arrival as 'Meena Kumari's hero' or wondered aloud whom he would star opposite next. Hari took these gibes sportingly. Years later, Saraiya would approach him while planning a remake of *Saraswatichandra* in Gujarati. This time Sanjeev Kumar would turn him down saying that a Hindi film actor shouldn't do films in other languages because it ruins his image. Saraiya realized the hurt he had caused the young actor years ago, and he cast Hari's younger brother Kishor Jariwala in the Gujarati film *Gun Sundari No Ghar Sansar* instead.

Imtiaz Khan, who was assisting K. Asif in the making of *Love and God* (also known as *Kais Aur Laila*, 1986), found an opportunity to direct *Zindagi Ki Raahein* after the director of the film quit. The film's lead actor, Sanjay Khan, was a friend of the previous director and he quit the movie as well. Imtiaz Khan was in a fix because he couldn't find an actor to replace Sanjay Khan. His brother Amjad Khan told him about Hari. When Imtiaz Khan asked Hari to step in, he immediately agreed to do so, no questions asked. However, Hari's run of bad luck was not over. The film was shelved due to a dispute between the producer and the financer. Not one to be subjugated by his circumstances, Hari continued looking for work.

He heard that V. Shantaram was looking for an actor to cast in his film *Geet Gaya Patharon Ne* (1964), and he headed out to ask him for work. Once again, the shabby kurta-pyjama stood between him and his success. Far from being impressed by Hari's appearance, V. Shantaram couldn't imagine how this person could aspire to become a hero. The director believed that a man dressed like Hari would not be able to do justice to a romantic hero's role. The role went to Jeetendra instead, and *Geet Gaya Patharon Ne* became his debut film.

While the big break Hari was looking for was still a long way off, small opportunities came his way now and then. When R.K. Nayyar was directing *Aao Pyar Karen* (1964) with Joy Mukherjee and Saira Banu, Hari and Mac Mohan bagged the roles of Joy Mukherjee's friends and received a monthly salary of Rs 125. The roles were small but significant, and even though Hari's six close-up shots were reduced to two, he was content with the outcome.

Since finances were dwindling, his friends nudged him to do a Gujarati film. Tarla Mehta, who was playing the female lead, along with Prabodh Joshi, the writer of the Gujarati film *Ramat Ramade Ram* (1964), pleaded with the director to cast Hari in the film. This turned out to be a good decision for Hari. He received Rs 1000 and, for the first time, starred in a song which was shot at Kamati Baug, Baroda, Gujarat.

One evening, Prabodh Joshi, Tarla Mehta, Mahesh Desai and Hari were sitting at Jaihind College, Churchgate, and discussing the on-screen names of eminent Bollywood artists. Hari declared that his name, Harihar Jariwala, was not befitting for an aspiring actor. While discussing the various possible names he could adopt, he decided that it should begin with the letter 'S', as his mother's name began with an 'S', and should end with 'Kumar' as most actors' names ended with 'Kumar'. After a gruelling debate and discussion, the name 'Sanjay Kumar' received unanimous approval, and Hari was credited in both *Ramat Ramade Ram* and *Aao Pyar Karen* by this name.

Now that his name was fixed, the only other thing that needed fixing was his appearance. Hari put away his trademark kurta pyjama and bought a red T-shirt and a pair of white trousers for interviews with directors and producers. This became an incentive for his friends to tease him whenever they saw him dressed in the red T-shirt and white trousers.

At Mac Mohan's sister's wedding, Hari met Anju Mahendru. She was with her friends and they were making fun of how Hari's appearance clashed with his aspirations. Anju decided to play a prank on Hari and asked him for an autograph. Hari took a paper napkin and kept writing until she became impatient and snapped:

I asked for an autograph, not a love letter.

Hari was merely responding to Anju's prank with his own. Thus began a friendship that would last a lifetime. Their bond strengthened while they were working on a film titled *Air Hostess*, which unfortunately never saw the light of day. Hari started visiting Anju at home. Her mother, Shanti Mahendru, grew so fond of him that she declared him her brother.

Hari's attachment to his humble roots endeared him to many. When a party at Anju Mahendru's house was interrupted by a large mouse, Hari was the only guest left unperturbed. When asked, he told the guests that he was used to mice in his Bhuleshwar residence. Sudhir Dalvi remembers Hari telling him that he could not sleep in his Pali Hill house for the first few days, missing the clanking of pots and pans and the sound of mice scurrying around.

Meanwhile, Hari continued with his efforts in getting a toehold in cinema. He invited producer–director Aspi Irani to watch one of his Gujarati plays at Tejpal Hall, Gowalia Tank, because he wanted to be a part of Irani's new film. Nargis Irani, Aspi Irani's sister, accompanied him, and recalls how her brother saw Hari on stage for the first time. He later asked her whether he should cast Hari in his film, and Nargis enthusiastically responded in the affirmative. And so, Hari was cast in Aspi Irani's *Badal* (1966).

Aspi was very close to producers J.B.H. Wadia and Homi Wadia. At that time, they were also planning to produce a new film under their banner Basant Pictures. The film was to be titled *Nishan* (1965), and Aspi had been signed on as director. Delighted with Hari's work in *Badal*, Aspi recommended him to the Wadias, and they signed him on for a monthly salary of Rs 250. Hari was so happy after he signed two films in quick succession that he took all his IPTA friends for dinner at Grand Road's Alamgir Hotel.

By a strange coincidence, child artiste Master Sachin had also been signed on by the Wadia brothers for the film *Zimbo Ka Beta* (1966), and Hari and Sachin started their Hindi film careers together from the same platform. Master Sachin would grow up to be the acclaimed actor Sachin Pilgaonkar and remain fast friends with Sanjeev Kumar. As Sachin said,

Zimbo Ka Beta's mahurat took place in the morning and Nishan's in the afternoon. In that sense, I was the first to enter Hindi films. First, however, does not mean more talented. Hari has already proven that he is one of the few talented actors we have in Hindi cinema.

Hari worked hard to meet everyone's expectations as a hero in *Nishan*. His dance director, Saroj Khan, fondly remembered his dedication and said that although he couldn't dance, he was extremely intelligent and improvised with gimmicks during song sequences. He would call her 'Masterji'.

She worked with him again later in *Naya Din Nayee Raat* (1974), *Mausam* (1975) and *Vidhaata* (1982), the last of which included a qawwali picturized on Sanjeev Kumar.

While Hari was shooting for *Nishan*, he met the versatile writer–producer–director Kamal Amrohi, who asked Hari to come over to Filmistan Studio Goregaon the following day to discuss two new films he was currently working on, *Aakhri Din Pehli Raat* and *Shankar Hussain* (1977).

Shankar Hussain was to be Hari's next project. When Hari went to meet Amrohi he was told to do a screen test with a few difficult dialogues in Urdu. The ever-diligent Hari delivered the dialogues in four different ways. Thoroughly impressed with Hari's confidence, Amrohi suggested that Hari work with his assistant Baqar to fine-tune his Urdu.

The hiccup with Hari's name came up again with Amrohi. The renowned director told him that his name was not impressive enough for an actor and decided to change Hari's screen name to Gautam Rajvansh and Vidya Manjrekar's (who initially played the protagonist's sister and later played the lead) to Al-Saheba. Both the actors accepted Amrohi's suggestion, and Hari refrained from telling him that he had already decided on Sanjay Kumar as his screen name.

Unfortunately, a day before the shooting was to start, the lead actress withdrew from shooting. Extremely caught up with *Pakeezah*

(1972), in which his wife Meena Kumari was playing a pivotal role, Amrohi shelved *Shankar Hussain* after a just few shots with Vidya as the new lead. As long as the shooting was on, however, Vidya Manjrekar remembers, Sanjeev Kumar was the most punctual man on the set, arriving even before the director and the rest of the crew to work on his dialogues. However, *Pakeezah* itself took years to produce and eventually everyone forgot about *Shankar Hussain* until Amrohi's son, Tajdar Kamal, decided to take it up again in 1977 with a different cast.

After Al-Saheba, Vidya's second screen name, Anjana, was decided by comedian–actor Mehmood. The name struck a chord with Vidya who became famous on screen as Anjana Mumtaz. Gautam Rajvansh and Al-Saheba of *Shankar Hussain* never appeared on celluloid or in the tabloids, but they both carved a niche for themselves in the Hindi film industry as Sanjeev Kumar and Anjana Mumtaz respectively.

Both *Badal* and *Nishan* were on the floor when Sanjay Khan's superhit film *Dosti* (1964) released and he instantly became a household name. Hari was in a dilemma yet again, since two Sanjays could not rule the screen at the same time. Aspi Irani advised him to alter his name once again. Hari was reluctant because two of his films had already been released as Sanjay Kumar. However, *Aao Pyar Karen* focused on Joy Mukherjee, and *Ramat Ramade Ram* was a regional film. He decided to take his chances, and Sanjeev Kumar was born.

Nishan was an average hit, and Sanjeev Kumar had become the hero of C-grade stunt films. After *Nishan*, he decided that he needed to work hard on his image and joined a gym called Shah Health Home at Princess Street.

Sanjeev Kumar grew close to Aspi Irani during the filming of *Badal* and *Nishan*. Aspi recommended him to Mehmood for *Pati Patni* (1966). Though the lead actress Nanda was said to be reluctant to perform with a stunt hero, she later clarified that this was a baseless rumour. In an interview, she said that she had asked Mehmood to cast the Marathi actor Kashinath Ghanekar. When Sanjeev's name was proposed, she agreed to work with him.

Sanjeev was very cooperative with all his directors. B.R. Ishara cast him in his debut film *Insaaf Ka Mandir* (1969) opposite a newcomer called Snehlata, and Aspi approached him once again for *Smuggler* (1966) and *Insaan Aur Shaitan* (1970). The budget for *Insaan Aur Shaitan* was limited, so he asked Madhumati, the female lead, and Sanjeev Kumar to bring their own clothes for the shoot. This led to a misunderstanding on the sets when Madhumati saw Sanjeev Kumar looking sharp in a suit for a shoot. She asked him where he got the clothes, and the mischievous Sanjeev told her that the producer had designed the costume for him since he was the hero. Hurt by this differential treatment, Madhumati approached Aspi, only to find out that he had loaned his suit to Sanjeev Kumar. When Aspi left, Sanjeev stepped up and showed her his handkerchief tucked neatly into his coat pocket and said:

This is not even a handkerchief—this is Bawa's sock . . .

And both of them were in splits.

B.R. Ishara's *Insaaf Ka Mandir* was shot at RK Studio, the same studio where Sanjeev used to stand outside the gate for hours looking for work. Again, Sanjeev provided evidence of both his skill and his hard-working approach to acting. The film features a scene with Sanjeev Kumar playing a lawyer and veteran actor Prithviraj Kapoor as the judge. It was a long- duration shot, with lengthy dialogues, and reshooting would cost a lot. There was a lot at stake. Sanjeev spent a long time rehearsing the dialogues. Rajendra Kumar, sitting in the sound department, criticized him, loudly claiming that he was unfit for the role. Sanjeev's pride was hurt, and he told Ishara that there was no need for further rehearsals. He completed the scene in one take. Mesmerized by his abilities, even Prithviraj Kapoor applauded him:

You are a genius—the film industry needs an actor like you!

Distinguished directors had started to notice Sanjeev Kumar, and Hrishikesh Mukherjee wanted to cast Sanjeev in his film *Anupama* (1966), but producer L.B. Lachhman refused because Sanjeev was still known as a C-grade film actor. The film went to Dharmendra instead. L.B. Lachhman made *Anokhi Raat* (1968) and *Arjun Pandit* (1976) with Sanjeev Kumar later, and Sanjeev received a Filmfare Best Actor award for *Arjun Pandit*.

Apart from the stunt roles, Sanjeev's roles in films like *Husn Aur Ishq* (1966), *Alibaba and 40 Thieves* (1966), *Aayega Aane Wala* (1967), *Gunehgar* (1967) and *Gunah Aur Kanoon* (1970) did nothing to improve his career or his finances. The eldest son in the family, he could no longer shrug off his responsibilities. He approached Pravin Joshi and requested a job at INT as an actor. However, this was not possible because actors at INT were called based on the requirement and paid according to their roles. To earn some money on the side, Sanjeev acquired a second-hand taxi and rented it out to a taxi driver, which doubled as a personal vehicle to take him to meetings with producers and directors.

Between trying to overwrite his status as a C-grade hero and finding many of his movies shelved, Sanjeev experienced a bout of depression. The films in which he had invested hope, like Kamran's *Badnam Farishte*, Aspi Irani's *Return of Qaidi No. 911*, S. Mehendi's *Ghar Ki Izzat*, Mahesh Kaul's *Hum Kahan Ja Rahe Hain*, Sameer Chaudhary's *Mitti Ke Dev*, Qamar Narvi's *Chand Phir Nikla* and Daya Kishan Sapru's *Jeevan Chalne Ka Naam,* had all been shelved.

When Hari learnt that B.R. Chopra was making a film titled *Aadmi Aur Insaan* (1969), he tried very hard to be a part of this venture to finally erase his C-grade image. He was in such a rush to get the film that he went to meet the Chopra brothers in his infamous kurta pyjama. Both B.R. Chopra and Yash Chopra refused to let him be a part of their film and the role went to Feroz Khan. Years later, they acknowledged that they had misjudged Sanjeev Kumar's talent and cast him in films like *Silsila* (1981), *Sawaal* (1982), *Trishul* (1978) and *Pati Patni Aur Woh* (1978).

Unaware of the success waiting for him just around the corner, Sanjeev Kumar felt overwhelmed with all the missed opportunities, all for little fault of his own. A despondent Sanjeev decided to shelve his dreams of becoming an actor and start looking for other means of income. Sudhir Dalvi remembers Sanjeev coming to him with a bar of gel soap and announcing:

> I don't think producers and directors need a talented actor. I am
> fed up of struggling. I have decided to get into the soap business.

Disheartened to see his optimistic friend so depressed, Sudhir convinced him to hang in there for a bit longer. He assured him that success would come to him, and soon.

6

Jamnadas's Sunghursh

Sanjeev heeded Sudhir's advice and decided to hold on for a bit longer. Yet, he was depressed and in a dilemma day in and day out. During this phase of hopelessness, a beacon of light shone his way in the form of *Sunghursh* (1968).

Producer–director H.S. Rawail was finding it difficult to get an actor who could hold his own against a giant like the superstar Dilip Kumar. Most well-known actors refused the role for fear of being overshadowed. So Rawail was on the lookout for someone talented and brave enough to not be daunted.

Sanjeev was confident that he had what it would take. But experience had taught him a hard lesson. With his reputation as a stunt actor, he knew he would be rejected if he personally approached Rawail. He asked his secretary, Jamnadas, to meet Rawail on his behalf.

Jamnadas was now a man on a mission. Rawail was a hard man to convince, but Jamnadas wasn't giving up easily. He visited Rawail's office at Famous Studio, Mahalaxmi, every alternate day, armed with Sanjeev Kumar's photographs and spoke at length about his natural gifts as an actor. Rawail tried to be polite and even assured Jamnadas that he would get in touch if there were any suitable roles for Sanjeev in the future, but Jamnadas wouldn't budge. He had to return to his friend and boss with some good news. Exasperated with Jamnadas's persistence, Rawail resorted to instructing his security guards to forbid him from entering the premises again. Poor Jamnadas was now utterly distraught. He waited for two whole days to visit Sanjeev again. When Sanjeev eventually asked him if he had spoken to Rawail, he could not bear to disappoint him, so he lied and said that Rawail was busy and had asked him to return the following week. What else could he have done?

That night, Jamnadas had an epiphany. Director Ramesh Saigal, at the helm of films like *Shaheed* (1948), *Phir Subah Hogi* (1958) and *Railway Platform* (1955), was Jamnadas's friend. He was also close to Rawail, with whom he played cards every once in a while. The following day, Jamnadas paid a visit to Saigal and spoke to him about Sanjeev. He left behind an envelope of Sanjeev's photographs. Saigal assured him that he would try his best, but the rest depended on the young hopeful's luck.

When Jamnadas left, Ramesh Saigal opened the envelope and was surprised to find the photographs of the young actor whose performance they had seen at Famous Studio, when the IPTA had hosted three one-act plays during the Navratri festival that year. Sanjeev Kumar had performed in a play titled *Baarah Bajkar Paanch Minute*. Rawail, who was in the audience, had found him to be a promising actor, but he remembered him as Harihar Jariwala. Rawail had even whispered to Saigal,

Jariwala has what it takes to become a great actor.

Over time, however, they had both forgotten him, which left Saigal in a pickle. How would he again bring up the subject with his friend?

Jamnadas, who would leave no stone unturned, came up with a brilliant plan. He arranged for two reels of under-production films where Sanjeev Kumar could be seen at his best. Saigal got in touch with Rawail and asked him to take a look at those films, on the pretext of helping him select an actor for an upcoming movie. Jamnadas booked them a preview theatre and both the reels were screened for Saigal and Rawail. Rawail approved of Sanjeev for Saigal's movie.

When Saigal and Rawail met in the evening, Saigal reminded him that this was the same actor whose performance had impressed them at the Navratri festival. But Rawail refused to believe him; he clearly remembered that the actor in question was called Jariwala. Saigal explained that he had changed his name for the screen, and Rawail knew at once that Sanjeev Kumar would be perfect for the role in *Sunghursh*. Sanjeev, meanwhile, had little idea of the lengths to which Saigal and Jamnadas had gone to get him the role that would prove to be pivotal for his career.

An expensive set depicting a haveli was constructed at Famous Studio and shooting for *Sunghursh* began. The day Sanjeev Kumar had been waiting for with bated breath had finally arrived. He was standing face to face with none other than Dilip Kumar.

Sanjeev knew how to keep calm. He had trained himself not to let excitement or nervousness get the better of him. When asked whether he was ready to shoot, he said yes with no hesitation.

In the scene, the two actors were to sit across from each other and play chess. As the cameras rolled, Dilip Kumar slipped effortlessly into his character and spoke his line, '*Chaal toh chalo, Thakur.*' Sanjeev was to look at him and convey the animosity his character felt. His expression was so well done that there was no need for a retake— no mean achievement for a newcomer sharing screen space with a megastar. The renowned poet–director Gulzar, who also wrote the dialogues for the film, was present as Rawail's assistant director, and he remembers the impact of Sanjeev's very first shot with 'Dilip Saheb'. For the second shot, the camera was placed over Sanjeev Kumar's shoulder to keep Dilip Kumar in the frame, and this time too, the shot was executed perfectly. Sanjeev Kumar had a small but challenging role, and he completed his shots in a remarkably short time.

Parikshat Sahni remembers his father Balraj Sahni coming home from shooting *Sunghursh* and saying:

Sanjeev is a great actor. Dilip Kumar and I like working with him.

Parikshat had not yet been introduced to Sanjeev, but in his first film *Anokhi Raat* (1968), he shared the screen with him. In *Anokhi Raat*, Sanjeev was playing a dacoit, while Parikshat had the role of an artist. As he remembers,

> When my father came to know about *Anokhi Raat* he invited Sanjeev to our bungalow at once, and opened a bottle of champagne to celebrate.

Balraj Sahni was immensely happy to see his son starting his career with Sanjeev, whom he loved like a son. Ajay Sahni's screen name, Parikshat Sahni, was also Sanjeev Kumar's suggestion.

Anokhi Raat's female lead, Zahida, Nargis Dutt's niece, was also one of many who did not expect much of Sanjeev Kumar. She first met him at the premiere of *Anupama* and wondered to herself what kind of a hero Sanjeev could be. When she started her career with *Anokhi Raat*, she had to face the camera for the first time with the same man, in a *suhaag raat* (wedding night) scene. The two became fast friends but did not have the opportunity to act together on screen again. Legend has it that Dilip Kumar was so taken aback with Sanjeev after his first shot with him in *Sunghursh* that he pulled Rawail aside and asked,

> *Iss ladke ko kahaan se pakad kar laaye ho?*

As the icon said later,

> What I said to Rawail was in a different tone . . . a man who was desperately in search of an actor for so many days had at last found one, so I casually asked him where he had found the boy.

He also went on to say that *Sunghursh* was not the first time that Sanjeev Kumar had appeared on his horizon. Many years ago,

Dilip Kumar, along with the famed actor–director–producer Sohrab Modi, had gone to watch a Gujarati play. Dilip Kumar had been spellbound the minute Sanjeev appeared on stage. He had inquired about him, and Sohrab Modi introduced Sanjeev as the 'famous Gujarati actor Harihar'. Moreover, Sanjeev Kumar was playing a role in the film *Sasta Khoon Mehnga Paani*, to be directed by K. Asif. Surely, Dilip Kumar must have been aware of Sanjeev Kumar the actor long before *Sunghursh*.

There was a huge buzz in the film industry after *Sunghursh*'s release, regarding Dilip Kumar's unwillingness to work in any film with Sanjeev Kumar. However, Dilip Kumar refutes this, saying that he did once refuse to work in the Sanjay Khan-starrer *Abdullah* (1980), in which Sanjeev Kumar appeared as well, but only because he was not satisfied with the script. He later worked with Sanjeev Kumar again in *Vidhaata* (1982).

In 1983, Sanjeev Kumar clarified his stance on *Sunghursh* in an interview with the author, published in the Hindi monthly magazine *Film Varsha*. He said:

> Only when the same role is played by two different actors can you compare the two. People wrote that in *Sunghursh* I was better than Dilip Kumar. Do you think this was right? I don't think so. People went to see *Sunghursh* for Dilip Kumar, not me. Yes, you can say that this actor is better than that actor, but you can't say Rajendra Kumar or Manoj Kumar is better than Dilip Kumar, because you can only judge them from their range. The fact is, Dilip Kumar is Dilip Kumar. Nobody can beat him.

Actor Deven Verma was also a part of *Sunghursh*, but he did not have the chance to perform with Sanjeev. Whenever Sanjeev faced the camera, Deven would watch his performance from the wings. Watching Sanjeev Kumar's performance on set became, by Deven's admission, a learning process for him. The most important thing he learnt was to concentrate on a given character without being bothered about who is sharing the screen with you.

On one occasion, during the making of *Sunghursh*, Sanjeev was sitting in Famous Studio and talking to Jamnadas. When Rawail entered and saw them deep in discussion, he could not help but ask Sanjeev if Jamnadas was his relative or cousin in addition to being his secretary. He went on:

> Whenever he approached me on your behalf, I insulted him, threw away your photographs, I even warned him not to enter my office. But he was persistent and he encouraged me to cast you. Only a father would do so much for a son, not a secretary.

Before this, Sanjeev had had only an inkling of how hard Jamnadas worked for him. Humbled, he replied:

> He is like a father to me.

Following this incident, Sanjeev Kumar always addressed him as 'Jamnadasji'.

7

Love, or Something like It

Nutan was slim, sharp-featured and stunningly beautiful. Her mother was the well-acclaimed Marathi film actress Shobhna Samarth. Shobhna played a vital role in every decision of Nutan's life and had directed her debut film, *Hamari Beti* (1950). Nutan had received part of her education in Switzerland and was a beauty pageant winner.

At the peak of her career, on 11 October 1959, Nutan married naval officer Lieutenant Commander Rajnish Bahl, the man she was in love with, in a grand ceremony. The first couple of years was marital bliss and soon they were blessed with a boy they named Mohnish. However, by the mid-1960s, the marriage hit a rocky patch. It was said, in hushed whispers, that Rajnish's word was the law in their household, that he held absolute authority and Nutan found his dominating nature suffocating.

According to reliable sources, it was Rajnish who coerced Nutan into dragging her mother to court. The notorious court battle soured Nutan's relationship with all her kin. Her siblings Chatura, Jaideep and Tanuja severed ties with her, and the mother–daughter relationship was ruined. Nutan was in despair, lonely and vulnerable. There was no one she could confide in, no person she could look to for guidance. It was during this turmoil that Nutan met Sanjeev Kumar.

Sanjeev and Nutan were working together in *Gauri* (1968) and *Devi* (1970). The more time Nutan spent with Sanjeev, the more she realized how soft-spoken and respectful he was. His tranquil demeanour was in complete contrast to the turbulence she faced at home. There was something soothing about his presence, and she found herself confiding in him. He became the friend she needed, a shoulder to cry on.

Sanjeev always advised Nutan to try to make her marriage work. But his well-meaning advice was failing to bridge the vast chasm between Nutan and Rajnish. After several attempts to fix their marriage, Nutan lost hope. In this phase of utter bleakness, she turned her affection to Sanjeev.

They fell in love with each other, but marriage was not on the cards. Being public figures, they could not meet in parks or at the beach. Producer–director Govind Saraiya, a mentor to both, often booked a hotel room for the two at Shalimar, Kemps Corner. They met in the room, but kept the doors open, pouring their hearts out to each other but never even so much as holding hands. When they were done talking, Saraiya would pick her up and she would return reluctantly to the reality of her marital life. Rajnish never suspected anything, as Saraiya was a family friend.

Nutan and Sanjeev's relationship soon became an open secret. Actor Arvind Joshi, Sanjeev's confidant from their days in Gujarati theatre, knew of their fondness for each other. Sanjeev often spoke to him of his desire to marry Nutan. He also recalls the frequent disputes in the Bahl household when Rajnish became aware of Sanjeev's involvement in Nutan's life. Anju Mahendru, another close friend, reminisces:

He was madly in love with Nutan-ji and he told me about his feelings for her. If Nutan-ji could have handled her differences with her husband, perhaps a marriage could have taken place.

The decision had to be taken mutually, and Nutan's consent was more important because she was trapped between her husband and her lover.

While news of Nutan and Sanjeev's love story spread like wildfire, Tarla Joshi knew how sincere Sanjeev was about the relationship.

Sanjeev was serious about her, and tried to remove Rajnish Bahl from her life. He bought her expensive gifts and even introduced me to her as his Nani Baa.

On one occasion, producer Mahesh Desai, close friend of Sanjeev Kumar, needed help getting a tax-free permit for his Gujarati film *Mahji Haiya* (1969). Desai approached Sanjeev to write a letter on his behalf and inadvertently witnessed an incident he would later recall many times over. At the time, Sanjeev Kumar happened to be shooting for a film with Nutan. Sanjeev couldn't find a pen to write the letter. When Nutan saw him rummaging around for something, she asked:

Aap kya dhund rahe ho? Aapko kisi cheez ki talaash hai? (What are you looking for? Do you need something?)

Sanjeev retorted:

Mujhe jis cheez ki talaash hai woh filhaal tum de nahi sakti, par ek pen la do? (What I am looking for is something you cannot give to me at present, but could you get me a pen for now?)

Nutan opened her purse for a pen. Before handing it to him, she said softly:

Ab bataiye jis cheez ki talaash hai aapko woh main de sakti hoon ya nahi? (Now, tell me, do you think I can't give you what you're looking for?)

An intimate conversation followed between the two, following which Sanjeev wrote the letter Mahesh Desai needed.

While everyone in town fuelled the rumours of their relationship, Shantaben did not know what was brewing in her son's life. Tarla Joshi decided to break the news to her. Shantaben knew how stubborn Sanjeev could be. If he had his heart set on Nutan, there was nothing anyone could do to dissuade him. She was aghast. Theirs was a respected family in the community, and his choice to love a married woman would not be accepted—furthermore, it would bring dishonour to their name. Tarla tried to console Shantaben saying that it was just a phase, but to no avail. After spending sleepless nights pondering her son's choices, Shantaben finally confronted Sanjeev, daring him to deny the rumours. Poor Sanjeev was caught in a dilemma. He was embarrassed to learn that his mother had found out about his love affair, and as the silence between them grew, Shantaben could sense that her worst fears were coming true. She counselled him to forget Nutan and look elsewhere for love and marriage. The respectful Sanjeev quietly heard her out, without replying harshly or arguing with his mother.

Tarla herself was torn between mother and son. On the one hand, she saw a heartbroken Sanjeev, and on the other, a distressed Shantaben. When asked if she ever tried to dissuade Sanjeev, she replied:

> It was not possible for me to stop it . . . if anyone pressured them to stop, the results would have been terrible for all.

Meanwhile, the Bahl household was in an uproar. Rajnish Bahl was a commander and was used to being unquestioningly obeyed. With his marriage teetering on the brink of slipping through his fingers, his rage knew no bounds. He interrogated Nutan ruthlessly every time she returned from work. The more he read and heard about Nutan and Sanjeev, the more violent his threats and treatment towards her became. Nutan tolerated everything quietly only because of her son—she couldn't bear to leave him.

In 1959, a person called Prem Ahuja was killed by his friend Kawas Manekshaw Nanavati, a naval officer and commander. Upon discovering Ahuja's illicit affair with his wife, Sylvia, Nanavati had taken a pistol from the naval base and had shot Ahuja thrice. Ahuja died on the spot. The case made headlines and, a few years later, Sunil Dutt made the film *Yeh Rastey Hain Pyar Ke* (1963) based on it. In an argument with Nutan, Rajnish brought the case up and threatened her with dire consequences if she kept up her association with Sanjeev.

In conversations with the author, Tarla Joshi, Anju Mahendru and Gayatri Patel have said that Rajnish's words chilled Nutan to the bone. For the first time she saw murder in his eyes, and she was certain he would follow through on his threat. Rajnish had lost his grip on his sanity. In another one of their arguments, he had dangled their son Mohnish from the window and had threatened to throw him out, returning to his senses only when mother and son screamed for each other. This was not an isolated incident. Anju Mahendru maintains that Rajnish was using Mohnish to blackmail his wife.

That night, a terrified Nutan locked herself in a room with her son. She had saved him from his father's rage this time. Would their luck hold out a second time? She decided that she could not take the chance. She had to sacrifice her relationship and save her marriage, if only for the sake of her young child. She made up her mind to make it publicly known once and for all that she would have nothing to do with Sanjeev Kumar. Her eyes swollen from crying, her face dark with anguish, her hair unkempt from neglect and her stride full of painful urgency, she made her way to Filmistan Studio. She made a beeline for Sanjeev sitting there and slapped him hard across the face. Child artiste Sarika, who later became a well-known actress in her own right, happened to have been sitting on his lap at the time. As Nutan slapped Sanjeev, her bangles shattered, and the pieces showered down on Sarika. Sanjeev's face bled. Subhash Indori rushed to stop Nutan as she was leaving, but Sanjeev held him back. Sarika had no idea what she had just witnessed.

Sanjeev's sister, Gayatri, however, claimed to know better. According to her, Nutan's relationship with her husband had already been strained before she met Sanjeev, and Sanjeev had merely tried to be a supportive friend. Perhaps the two had fallen in love at some point. But a day before this incident, Sanjeev had called Rajnish to explain the situation to him and clear the air of the ugly rumours. Sanjeev's well-meant call became the cause for a huge fight in the Bahl household, and, unable to control her anger, Nutan slapped Sanjeev. At no point, says Gayatri, did her brother ever discuss Nutan with her, and Nutan never visited the Jariwalas at their residence.

Ruby Irani remembers Sanjeev coming from Filmistan to Nepean Sea Road later to see her husband, Aspi Irani. Aspi advised Sanjeev to not mention the incident to anyone. Although advised to call a press conference, Sanjeev did not do so. Even as he grieved his lost love, Sanjeev Kumar put up a stoic front, and only his close friends knew of his acute heartache.

After a couple of years, rumours started doing the rounds of Sanjeev being involved with Nutan's sister Tanuja. In an interview with Ameen Sayani in the 1970s, Sanjeev Kumar spoke about Tanuja:

> My first best friend is a young girl named Tanuja. I am like a father to her, Ameen Bhai. I don't know what it is about her, but every time I look at her, I feel differently about her. Sometimes I see her as my sister and feel protective of her; when I take my problems to her, she advises me as someone much older would . . . and sometimes she behaves like my daughter.

At the time, he was playing Tanuja's father in *Oos Raat Ke Baad* (1970). There was nothing romantic between the two—they differed widely in their views on marriage. As Sanjeev went on to say:

> I always feel that my wife should be at home and take care of the kids, but that's not how Tanuja thinks . . . I don't think Tanuja can even imagine living the way I expect my wife to live.

Sanjeev was sure that he would not marry an actress, and if he did, he would not want her to continue facing the camera after marriage.

Nutan broke her silence on her friendship with Sanjeev Kumar after he passed away. In an interview with Gautam Rajadhyaksha for *Junior G*, she declared:

> I was a busy actress and happy with my career and family. I always kept my distance from the gossip columns, but I could not stop two stories from coming out—one on the dispute between my mother and me . . . the other that I had slapped Sanjeev Kumar.

When Nutan and Sanjeev parted ways, Tarachand Barjatya decided to drop Sanjeev Kumar from the film *Saudagar* (1973). The shooting was supposed to begin in 1969 and, according to Sudhir Dalvi, it was Nutan who had recommended Sanjeev for the film. Later, this film was made with Amitabh Bachchan and Nutan. Producer–director Govind Saraiya had also been planning to make *Agnipariksha* with Nutan and Sanjeev. The story was closely based on Nutan and Rajnish's marriage, as Saraiya knew them quite closely, but due to Nutan and Sanjeev's problems, the film was never made.

A well-known actor from that era, who also happened to be Sanjeev Kumar's friend, planned a special surprise party for him after Nutan ended their friendship. He organized a get-together at a five-star hotel and invited all their actor friends. When Sanjeev reached the party, the host asked him to stand in the middle of the room and instructed every actor to come and kiss Sanjeev on the cheek that Nutan had slapped. Sanjeev couldn't help but blush and smile. He might have lost Nutan's love, but he had gained the love of many others.

8

The Big Break . . . Success at Last

The Indian film industry, like all other commercial enterprises, is highly result-driven. Either you're a hit or you're not: there's no in-between. Sanjeev Kumar was no stranger to this fact. That he was amply talented had already been established by his performance in *Sunghursh*. However, the film was not a box-office hit, and Sanjeev was desperately looking for an opportunity that would bill him as a commercial success and cement his position in the industry.

A well-known adage in India goes, *Daane daane par likha hai khaanewale ka naam* (every morsel of food carries the name of its consumer), which can be modified to the film industry as, role role *par likha hai nibhanewale ka naam* (every role has its predestined actor).

L.V. Prasad's *Khilona* (1970), based on Gulshan Nanda's novel *Patthar Ke Hont*, was conceptualized with Guru Dutt in mind. When L.V. Prasad heard that Dutt was caught up with K. Asif's *Love and God*, he decided to postpone the project. Unfortunately, Guru Dutt passed away before *Love and God* was finished, one of the many incidents that would lead to the film being dubbed one of the most ill-fated movies ever made in the industry. L.V. Prasad was left in the lurch.

After a lot of deliberation, Sanjeev Kumar was zeroed in on as a perfect replacement for Dutt. He had already played the role in a Gujarati adaptation called *Maare Jaav Pehle Paar*, for which he had won the Gujarat State Award for Best Actor. Besides, Prasad had seen Sanjeev's commitment to the craft first-hand during the filming of *Raja Aur Runk* (1968) and *Jeene Ki Raah* (1969).

Khilona was being made with the utmost care. Author Gulshan Nanda wrote the screenplay, in consultation with the renowned writer Agha Jani Kashmiri. Intensive research had been carried out on mental health imbalances, since the protagonist was to lose his mind after witnessing a shocking incident. Assistant director Prakash Kapoor was sent to the Thane Mental Hospital to study some cases. It took seventeen months to complete the script. Sanjeev brought his own experiences to the character, basing part of it on a man he had met in Surat who suffered from a fear of fire. Shatrughan Sinha, Jeetendra, Dheeraj Kumar and Mumtaz were using every connection they had to get a role in this movie. Prasad cast Jeetendra in a supporting role as he had already worked with Sanjeev in *Jeene Ki Raah*. Shatrughan Sinha bagged the negative role of Bihari, and Leena Chandavarkar was supposed to play the female lead. However, her fee exceeded the film's budget, and the role of Chand went to Mumtaz, who was willing to do it for Rs 90,000. The largest sum, of Rs 2 lakh, was paid not to an actor but to the cameraman Dwarka Divecha, and Sanjeev received a payment of Rs 1,20,000. The music composer duo Laxmikant–Pyarelal decided to rope in Mohammed Rafi as the playback singer for Sanjeev Kumar. Pyarelal later mentioned:

There were very few actors who had no particular playback singer attached to their image. Sanjeev Kumar was one of them. Mukesh, Manna Dey, Kishore Kumar, Mohammed Rafi, Mahendra Kapoor and even Bhupendra had sung for him as his voice matched all of them.

A special set was made at RK Studio and the film's shooting began in full swing. Outsiders were not allowed on the set. The film ran into problems when, halfway through the making, the director felt that Shatrughan Sinha might have been the wrong choice for the role of Bihari. When he tried to replace him, however, his colleagues Sanjeev and Mumtaz rushed to his defence. Their unwavering loyalty proved to be the start of a lifelong friendship. Sanjeev himself was often in trouble for being late to the sets. As assistant director Prakash Kapoor remembers,

> The shooting was held back for Sanjeev. L.V. Prasad was very upset as everyone was already on the set. When Sanjeev came, Prasad didn't say anything to him, but after pack-up he called me aside and asked me to tell him that this should not be repeated.

Not one to be told twice, Sanjeev was not late to the sets again.

It was time to shoot one of the pivotal scenes for the film. His character Vijay was to lose his mind at the sight of firecrackers. This was a particularly difficult shot; not only was it long, but it was also riddled with intricate nuances that would test his mettle as an actor. Sanjeev, true to form, completed the scene in one take and, impressed, Prasad told him,

> If you want to come late for the shoot I don't mind, but please inform me in advance.

During the shooting of *Khilona*, Sanjeev struck a friendship with cameraman Dwarka Divecha, who had nicknamed him '*Gujarat no Gando*' (Madman of Gujarat). Sanjeev would patiently stand for hours under the spotlight to help Divecha find the right angle and lighting condition for the scene. Finally, the shoot was complete. Months of research had gone into the writing of *Khilona*, but the shooting was completed within just seven months.

The film released and Sanjeev Kumar was established as a star. He was featured on the cover of every notable film magazine and was inundated with offers to play similar roles. Sanjeev and Jamnadas refused all of them, except for the suspense thriller *Anhonee* (1973), which cast him as a police inspector pretending to be mentally ill to catch a culprit.

The massive success of *Khilona* was something Sanjeev had no experience of. The film was a superhit at the box office, and it went on to receive six Filmfare Awards nominations in 1971. It won two of these—Best Film and Best Actress for Mumtaz. The big break Sanjeev Kumar was looking for had finally arrived, and all his insecurities about his position in the industry were laid to rest once and for all.

The success of *Khilona* opened doors for him and he was flooded with meaningful offers, varied and infinitely more prestigious than the stunt films he had taken up to make a living. It helped him purchase a car and a house at Pali Hill, one of the poshest locations Bombay could offer, although he held on to his house in Bhuleshwar.

Writer-turned-director Rajinder Singh Bedi was working on his radio play *Naql-e-Makaani* (Moving to a New House) to turn it into a film. Prompted by his son, Narendra Bedi, who had worked with Sanjeev previously for *Bandhan*, he was considering Sanjeev Kumar for the role of the protagonist, Hamid. Sanjeev also came highly recommended by the veteran actor A.K. Hangal. *Khilona* hadn't released by then and Bedi had little idea about who Sanjeev Kumar truly was, but he decided to act upon his son's and Hangal's recommendations and sign him for his film *Dastak* (1970).

The film had an unusual storyline, following the lives of a couple who rent an apartment previously owned by a sex worker. The casting was up in the air. Although Mumtaz, fresh from playing Sanjeev's co-star in *Khilona*, wanted the role, the director refused to cast her. She looked too innocent to play the unabashed Salma, and Bedi had Leela Naidu in mind for the role.

Before the filming began, Rajinder Singh Bedi went to the Film and Television Institute of India in Pune to deliver a talk on acting. Jaya Bhaduri, Rakesh Pandey, Sadhu Meher, Radha Saluja and Rehana Sultan were all students at the institute. While a few students' films were being played for Bedi, he noticed a young girl playing the role of a pregnant woman standing in line for her chance to fill her bucket at the community tap. Her sultry appearance caught his eye, and Bedi realized that he had found his Salma. Her name was Rehana Sultan, and he decided that she would replace Leela Naidu. As per institute rules, she could not shoot unless she completed her acting course, and Bedi decided to wait for her. Shooting began at the Kamalistan Studio, also known as Kamal Amrohi Studio, soon after Rehana was done with her course. The film was being made on a low budget, so only two make-up rooms were allotted for the lead actors, both male and female. The rest of the cast had to sit under a tree and get their make-up done. Sanjeev was pleasantly surprised to find that his make-up room was spectacularly decorated with Rajasthani curios, plush sofas and a comfortable bed; a huge portrait of Meena Kumari hung on one of the walls. There was also a Filmfare Award for Best Actress, which Meena Kumari had won for *Parineeta* (1953). Sanjeev realized that he was standing in Meena Kumari's personal make-up room, built for her by her husband, Kamal Amrohi, the famous director and founder of the studio. A big fan of Meena Kumari, he couldn't resist picking up her award and staring at his reflection in the mirror with it. He had already won the Filmfare Award for Best Supporting Actor for Atma Ram's *Shikar* (1968), but the desire to win something of this calibre was a fire in his belly. The next day, when he returned to the studio, he found the make-up room closed and padlocked. He learnt that the room had accidentally been left open the previous day, and that it was out of bounds for everyone under strict orders from Amrohi.

Disheartened, Sanjeev decided to share Rehana Sultan's make-up room, which was not very spacious and had only one sofa.

Rehana compromised for the first couple of days, getting her make-up done under the tree like the other artistes, but her patience soon wore thin and she objected about the situation to the director. She stated very clearly that she wouldn't continue shooting if she didn't get her make-up room back. Everyone from assistant director Z.B. Lahiri to director Rajendra Singh Bedi himself tried to persuade her to drop the issue, but she was adamant. However, when Sanjeev Kumar approached her and politely requested her to let him use her make-up room, she caved, unable, by her own admission, to resist his charming smile.

Sanjeev Kumar also helped Rehana Sultan when her film *Chetna* (1970), with B.R. Ishara, seemed to be slipping through her fingers because of her prior commitment to *Dastak*, personally assuring Ishara that the shooting dates wouldn't clash.

A particular scene in *Dastak*, however, although apparently simple, was proving to be quite a challenge to film. Salma's younger sister was to inadvertently burst into the room when Salma was in bed with her husband. A young girl desperate to experience love, she was to break down upon seeing her sister being intimate with a man. Realizing why her sister was crying, Salma exchanges a meaningful glance with her husband. Rehana, however, was unable to grasp the subtle layers of emotions which Salma and her sister were experiencing. Director Bedi, too, couldn't find the right words to explain the nuances of the moment, and he only told Rehana to play it as a sister comforting her sister. Rehana started growing nervous as five retakes stretched to ten.

Finally, Sanjeev stepped in. With permission from Bedi, he proceeded to direct the scene himself. First, he asked everyone who was not required for the scene to leave the set. To give Rehana an emotional reference, he told her to imagine that something important had been stolen from her house, and she had to convey how she felt only through her eyes. The scene was completed without any more retakes. Rehana remembers Sanjeev as a kind, respectful man who treated the scene with the utmost delicacy:

A young Sanjeev Kumar dressed up as Krishna

Sanjeev Kumar provided a strong supporting act in the Rajesh Khanna-starrer
Aap Ki Kasam

Giving the clap for the mahurat of the film *Tanariri*

Another successful film in the actor's oeuvre, *Chehre Pe Chehra*, which gave him the opportunity to display his histrionic abilities

The romantic gaze; Sanjeev Kumar and Sulakshana Pandit in a still from *Chehre Pe Chehra*

Sanjeev Kumar with his mother, Shantaben Jariwala, at an award function in Delhi

A still from *Hamare Tumhare*; Sanjeev Kumar and Rakhee starred in quite a few family melodramas in the 1970s

An emotional Sanjeev Kumar during the *bidaai* ceremony of his sister, Gayatri. Also pictured is his brother-in-law, Ashok Patel

With Reena Roy in *Ladies Tailor*

A candid moment between Sanjeev Kumar and his sister, Gayatri, during his birthday celebrations

With Amitabh Bachchan and Jaya Bhaduri, both of whom starred in a number of films with Sanjeev Kumar

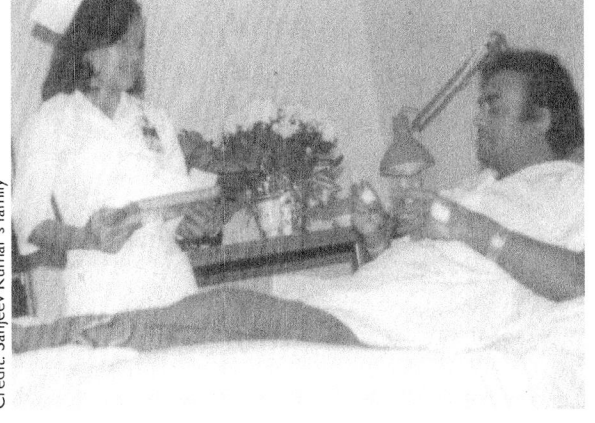

Sanjeev Kumar when he was admitted to a hospital in the United States of America

With Rajendra Kumar

With Reena Roy,
another actress with
whom Sanjeev Kumar
starred in a few films

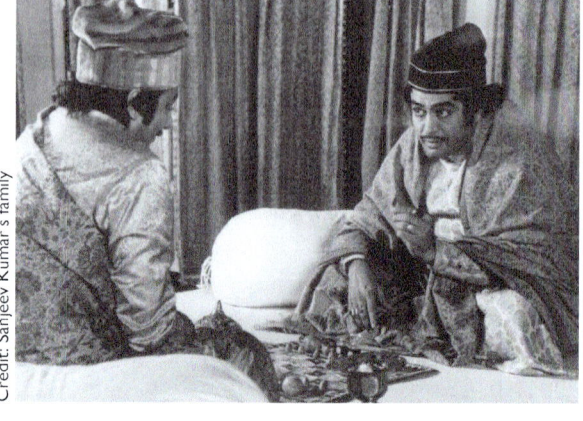

Saeed Jaffrey and
Sanjeev Kumar
in Satyajit Ray's
Shatranj Ke Khilari

Credit: Indian Cinema Heritage Foundation

On the set of *Takkar*, with Mac Mohan, Jeetendra and Ranjeet

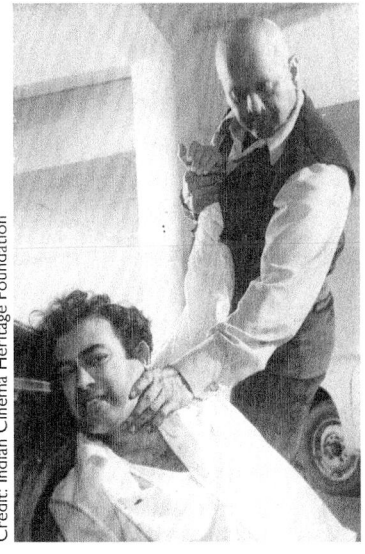

Credit: Indian Cinema Heritage Foundation

Credit: Indian Cinema Heritage Foundation

A still from *Anhonee*; Sanjeev Kumar was never quite the action star, but his aura ensured that he pulled off that genre too

His presence enabled him to stand out in a variety of roles; seen here in a still from *Aakraman*

The look that spoke
a thousand words;
a still from *Aandhi*

Be it a law-enforcement
officer (as in the still on the
right, from *Be-Reham*) or a
petty crook (below, still from
Waqt Ki Deewar), Sanjeev
Kumar brought to life every
character he played.

He was the hero and he could have explained it to me openly but
he did not. He did not even mention this in any of his interviews.

This reputation of a man always respectful to women followed Sanjeev
throughout his career. When Rehana was shooting for *Dastak* with
Sanjeev in Pune, she was the only female artiste in a room full of
make-up men and spot boys. They were working in a small room and
as soon as the director declared 'Pack up!' everyone trickled out to
the terrace. Everyone except Rehana. No one invited her, making her
feel rather left out. She decided to follow Sanjeev and join them, but
Sanjeev asked her not to because it was meant only for 'adults'. She
felt terrible but later discovered that he had only done so to protect
her, since the men were drinking on the terrace.

Sanjeev received the National Award for Best Actor for his
performance in *Dastak*, presented by the honourable President of
India V.V. Giri himself. Sanjeev took his mother and brother Kishore
along to receive the award. *Dastak* proved to be a turning point for
Rehana Sultan as well because she bagged the Best Actress award,
a remarkable achievement as a debutante. Rehana remembers with
great affection that Sanjeev had called to inform her that she had won
the National Award, explaining to the young woman that it was an
honour equal to an Academy Award.

This award finally opened the eyes of the Patel community,
who had so far shunned the Jariwalas for flouting the rules they held
sacred. They had vociferously objected to Shantaben's involvement
in matters of business and had also looked down upon Sanjeev's
preoccupation with acting. But his award changed their outlook and
they felicitated Sanjeev Kumar with the Surat Jilla Leuva Patidar
Gnyati Award on 4 April 1971. While receiving the trophy, Sanjeev
Kumar gave a brief speech:

This trophy is for my mother, Shantaben, since I am what I
am because of her. After the death of my father Jethalal, no
one stepped up to take care of our business and family, but she

single-handedly took over our business, against the wishes of the entire Gujarati community, and instantly became my inspiration. She constantly encouraged me to have patience and keep fighting to overcome my struggles. I am forever grateful to my mother, and I am also thankful to my community for felicitating me.

9

Love and God: Forever in the Making

Film tabloids have always followed fallouts between erstwhile friends in the industry with an obsessive curiosity. The rift between two of the biggest names in the industry—Dilip Kumar and K. Asif— naturally drew a great deal of attention.

K. Asif directed his friend Dilip Kumar in his magnum opus *Mughal-E-Azam* (1960), but they parted ways just before the release of the epic film, when Asif married Dilip Kumar's sister. Dilip Kumar refused to bless the union, because Asif was already a married man when he tied the knot with the superstar's sister.

After the grand success of *Mughal-E-Azam*, K. Asif began to work on his dream project *Love and God*, based on the tragic romance of Laila and Majnu. He knew that Dilip Kumar wouldn't agree to be a part of his venture, so he decided to cast Guru Dutt as Majnu and Nimmi as Laila. Nimmi took up the project, assuming that the film would endow her with everlasting fame, just as *Mughal-E-Azam* had done for Madhubala. Perhaps it would even prove to be a befitting swan song before her retirement. Guru Dutt, however, was not convinced. Right after the mahurat at Mohan Studios, Andheri, Dutt expressed his doubts to Asif, saying that he did not look like Majnu at all. Asif reassured him, telling him that he fit the director's

vision of the film perfectly. Even as the shooting started and Guru
Dutt donned Majnu's costume, he repeated to Asif that he would
not be able to do justice to the character. But Asif insisted they
continue.

Little did they know at the launch of the project in 1962 that
it would be another twenty-four years before the film would be
completed and released. In 1986, a distorted, unfinished version of
Love and God was released for public viewing. By then, both the
heroes and the director had passed away.

The film was doomed from the start, driven aground by the
director's stubborn refusal to compromise. Guru Dutt had already
attempted suicide twice, foiled both times by his domestic help.
The actor was going through a tremendous crisis. His marriage with
Geeta Dutt was on the rocks. Geeta Dutt had moved out of their
home with their three children. Weighed down by further financial
troubles, he had had to give up their house. Abandoned by all, Dutt
slipped steadily into depression and alcoholism. Meanwhile, the split
was taking its toll on his wife as well; Geeta paid little attention to her
singing career as she too drowned her sorrows in the bottle. Imtiaz
Khan, the assistant director of *Love and God*, felt that Guru Dutt's
forebodings were justified in his reluctance to work with a reputed
director like K. Asif.

Unaware of the turmoil his hero was in, Asif began appointing
painters and set designers to create a backdrop of heaven for his
film's climax. Ram Kumar, the chief painter, was given directions by
Asif himself. Heaven had to be created exactly as Asif envisioned it.
A tough taskmaster, Asif saw heaven as a picturesque garden with
blossoming flowers of every shade, nestling doves, fluttering butterflies
and dancing peacocks. *Love and God* had to surpass the opulence of
Mughal-E-Azam and no mistake would be tolerated. Some days, he
took only one shot. With little concern for time or budget, he kept
asking for retakes until he was satisfied with the outcome.

On the night of 9 October 1962, Guru Dutt had another fight
with his wife over their children. He drank the night away. Coupled

with his dangerous addiction to sleeping pills, his second bottle proved to be his last. The next morning his physician arrived to find a locked door.

Following their fight, Geeta Dutt had spent a restless night. She had a premonition that something terrible was coming their way. She wanted to go to his place that very night, but her mother held her back due to the lateness of the hour. The next morning, when she received frantic calls telling her that Guru Dutt wasn't opening the door, she told them to break it open. They followed her orders and found his lifeless body on the bed. Whether Guru Dutt's death was a suicide or an accident, no one could tell for sure.

His sudden death sent shock waves across the country, forcing *Love and God* to come to a grinding halt. Asif wouldn't continue with the film if he didn't have complete faith in the capabilities of the actors. Guru Dutt, in Asif's eyes, was perfect for the role of Majnu, and no one could replace him.

A few years later, K. Asif bumped into Sanjeev Kumar at a movie preview. They exchanged pleasantries while Sanjeev was looking for his shoes, but that short span of time was enough for Asif to recognize Sanjeev's potential. He didn't offer him *Love and God* straightaway; instead, he proposed to him a role in *Sasta Khoon Mehnga Pani* with Rajendra Kumar, Saira Banu and Jayant. The shooting took them into the deserts of Rajasthan. While Asif was busy with Rajendra Kumar and Saira Banu, he paid scant attention to poor Sanjeev stewing in the sun, in heavy make-up and uncomfortable costumes. He waited for hours in the scorching heat, but his turn never came. After spending almost twenty days in those agonizing conditions without facing the camera, he decided to raise the issue with the production controller, Ramzan, who conveyed it to K. Asif. Far from showing concern, Asif retorted that this was not his problem. If the legendary Dilip Kumar could not overrule him, neither could Sanjeev Kumar. According to Asif:

I came here to make films, not to solve problems.

When Asif's retort was relayed to Sanjeev Kumar, he didn't retaliate because he was well aware of Asif's short temper. He decided to simply finish the shoot and return to Bombay as soon as possible. He sat, uncomplainingly in the baking heat, awaiting his turn. After days, he was informed that it was the last day of the shoot and that Rajendra Kumar was leaving for Bombay that very evening. He was perplexed. There seemed to be no way that he could be a part of the movie any more. Just before the crew packed up for good, Asif summoned Sanjeev and took two shots, one long and the other a mid-shot. The actor was baffled. He felt cheated. Had he come all this way for no reason? Without wasting any more time on what looked like a hopeless cause, he returned to Bombay with the rest of the crew.

What Sanjeev did not know was that Asif had been testing his mettle, to find out if he had what it took to be the lead actor of *Love and God*. The gruelling hours spent under the blistering sun were essential to see if Sanjeev could portray the role of Majnu. The sheer desperation, exhaustion and anxiety that would feature on Majnu's face were reflected perfectly on Sanjeev's. Not only did he look like the Majnu Asif had visualized, but he had also demonstrated that he could endure hardships. Shooting in the desert wasn't going to be a cakewalk, but Sanjeev had proved that he had the patience and the perseverance to see it through.

Soon, K. Asif announced to the media that he had finally found his Majnu for *Love and God*—Sanjeev Kumar—and Sanjeev understood the reason for his travails. Thus, *Love and God* resumed shooting in 1969, five years after it had abruptly stopped.

Prior to the shooting of *Love and God*, Asif imposed strict restrictions on Sanjeev Kumar's diet. Quite willingly, Sanjeev put aside his habit of drinking every evening. Working with a director of this stature was a matter of great prestige, and Sanjeev was ready to do whatever it took. The perfectionist Asif took to driving to Sanjeev's house at midnight to check on him, to make sure he wasn't slipping. However, after a couple of unannounced visits, he realized that it was extremely ill-mannered on his part to disturb Sanjeev's entire household in the dead of night, so he booked a room for Sanjeev at Shalimar Kemps Corner (the same room where Sanjeev used to meet Nutan) and employed four guards to keep an eye on him. He also appointed Dr Jassawala to look into Sanjeev's diet and well-being. Dr Jassawala prescribed a massage, some exercises and steam baths. He also instructed him about what to eat and how much. Even his daily cups of tea were monitored!

A committed professional, Sanjeev complied with all of Asif's demands, as Govind Saraiya remembers. Nimmi also occasionally visited his hotel to see how Sanjeev was preparing, and was impressed with how much he was enduring to fulfil Asif's dream. His numerous friends, used to seeing him as a man who enjoyed his food and drink, were surprised to see his willingness to change for this prestigious role. As Mahesh Desai remembers, Sanjeev Kumar told him that he was feeling weak and dizzy, but he wanted to do *Love and God* at any cost, it being a K. Asif creation.

Perhaps Sanjeev Kumar was banking on this movie to be his magnum opus. Dilip Kumar had *Mughal-E-Azam*, Guru Dutt had *Pyaasa* (1957), Raj Kapoor had *Awara* (1951), Nargis had *Mother India* (1957) and Meena Kumari had *Sahib Biwi Aur Ghulam* (1962). *Love and God* would be his. The movie had all the ingredients of a classic and, if done right, his name was sure to go down in history. This belief was his driving force, giving him the strength to forfeit all pleasures. Eventually, all this hard work paid off and Sanjeev lost a lot of weight—so much so that nobody could recognize him at a glance.

As soon as Sanjeev's physique matched the requirements of the film, work for *Love and God* began once again. For Sanjeev Kumar's make-up, Asif hired the same artist who had worked for him in *Mughal-E-Azam*, and he himself sat with the make-up artist to preside over the look. It took six hours to do his make-up. When Sanjeev Kumar finally stepped outside, with a bowl in his hand, no one could recognize him any more. Legend has it that Asif proudly proclaimed:

Yeh hai mera Majnu, aur Majnu aisa hota hai. (This is my Majnu, and this is what Majnu looks like.)

On being asked who was more suited to the role, Nimmi replied that the filming with the two stars had happened with a gap of five years, and so it was hard for her to judge who was better. However, she could say with some degree of certainty that Sanjeev took more interest in the character than Guru Dutt had done. While shooting, both her leading men had become her friends, and she lamented:

> I still miss them.

Sanjeev and Asif soon became close friends. They met regularly at Sanjeev's place and discussed movies for hours. They discovered that they had a lot in common. They smoked the same brand of cigarettes and held their cigarettes the same way; they were both foodies at heart and enjoyed scrumptious, non-vegetarian dishes. The strangest and most poignant similarity, to surface later, was that they both passed away in Parin Villa at more or less the same age.

The two grew so close that Asif referred to Sanjeev as his younger brother. On one instance, during the shooting of *Love and God*, they visited the shrine of Khwaja Garib Nawaz in Ajmer. While they were sitting there, lost in their thoughts, a passer-by recognized them and stopped to ask Asif if the man sitting beside him was the hero Sanjeev Kumar. When quizzed further, Asif said with assurance that Sanjeev was his brother. Taken aback, the stranger asked him how this could be, since Asif was a Muslim and Sanjeev, a Hindu. Unperturbed, Asif smiled and said this was precisely why he thought of him as his very own.

In a radio interview with Ameen Sayani in 1974, Sanjeev Kumar said:

> Asif Sahib had a huge influence over me. If my mother wanted me to do something, she would ask Asif Sahib to talk me into it. She even requested him to force me to get married, but Asif Sahib

asked my mother to let him first complete *Love and God*, and once that was over, he would get me married at his own expense. My mother laughed and told him that by then I would be too old to get married.

On 9 July 1970, Sanjeev threw a lavish birthday party at Juhu Hotel and invited all his friends, including K. Asif, who arrived with a massive gift, covered in a blue cloth, carried by four people. Everyone was all agog to know what Asif had brought for Sanjeev. Surely, such a massive gift would be something priceless. After a great deal of suspense, when the blue cloth was removed with a flourish, all it revealed was sand. Asif had played a prank on Sanjeev, leaving all the guests in splits. Inimitably, however, he had inscribed the words *Love and God* on the sand.

Asif was spending a good deal of time and money on *Love and God*. He had arranged for over 200 junior artistes for Laila's marriage scene. Meanwhile, assistant director Imtiaz Khan declared that he didn't want to continue to work with K. Asif any longer as he was busy with other projects. Asif requested Imtiaz's brother, Amjad Khan, already a part of the movie, to replace him. Fortunately, Amjad and Sanjeev had been friends from their theatre days. They grew closer during the making of *Love and God*, chatting on the sets for hours, with one shared cigarette passing between them.

While shooting for *Love and God* in Rajasthan, Asif decided to pay a visit to Hazrat Sufi Hamiduddin Baba's dargah at Nagaur. Lost in his prayers, he saw a saint-like figure appear out of nowhere, who advised him not to attempt to create God's heaven in his film. It said:

Heaven can only be made by God. If you don't follow my instruction you will have to face consequences.

When Sanjeev heard of this he was shaken. However, Asif decided to pay no heed to it and continued making a set of heaven for his film.

In the first week of March 1971, Sanjeev Kumar left for Madras for a shoot of *Man Mandir* (1971), and K. Asif missed him sorely. No one knows why he felt so anxious and disturbed—it was as if he was having a premonition similar to what Guru Dutt had experienced all those years ago. He made a trunk call to Madras from Bombay and spoke to his friend to soothe himself. He instructed Sanjeev to call him for at least two minutes every day irrespective of his location, and to visit him the moment he reached Bombay.

Sanjeev did as he was told. As soon as he landed in Bombay on 8 March, he went to see Asif and stayed talking with him late into the night. Asif's ex-wife, Sitara Devi, was to meet him the next day, which got postponed to 10 March. Nimmi was also supposed to meet Asif on 9 March. When she reached his house, his wife, Akhtar, told her that he had just left to meet Dilip Kumar at Pali Hill, so she waited. Dilip Kumar's brother Ahsan Khan remembers Asif visiting him briefly before leaving for Sanjeev's. There seemed to be nothing unusual about his behaviour.

When Asif reached Parin Villa, he sat with Sanjeev in the glass room, where Sanjeev usually entertained, and they discussed their project. Sanjeev's mother, Shantaben, his brother, Nikul, and Jamnadas were also at home. His sister, Gayatri, was out shopping.

Suddenly, Shantaben heard Sanjeev frantically calling out for her. Jamnadas and she rushed into the room. Asif was struggling to breathe. Sanjeev asked Jamnadas to call Dr Gandhi, their family doctor, immediately. Nikul and Sanjeev tried to help Asif to Sanjeev's bed, but they could do little. As he breathed his last, Asif whispered:

Allah maut de toh sher ki de—tadpa ke mat maarna! (Allah, if death is what you have in mind for me, give me the death of a tiger— please don't make me suffer.)

As his friend died in his arms, Sanjeev Kumar reeled with shock. Dilip Kumar and Akhtar had to be informed. Nimmi was still with Akhtar when they received a call from Sanjeev informing them that

Asif was gravely ill. They left immediately but by the time they arrived, he had passed away.

Gayatri Patel recalls seeing a large crowd near their building. She rushed in, terrified that something had happened to their mother, but inside she noticed Dilip Kumar in a sombre mood and Akhtar weeping inconsolably. She realized what had transpired. Their families were very close. Gayatri remained with Akhtar for a week after her husband's untimely death.

Sanjeev had lost yet another father figure. He told Ameen Sayani of the uncanny resemblance of this episode to his father's death. Years ago, his father too had died in Hari's bed. He was devastated, but Asif's death spurred him on to complete his unfinished movie, and he even enlisted Dilip Kumar's help in doing so.

Sanjeev's nephew Uday Jariwala was a young boy at the time, but he still remembers his dada sitting in a rocking chair next to a large photograph of K. Asif:

> He used to sit and stare at that photograph a lot. Once, he picked me up in his lap and showed me the photograph, saying 'Beta, he is my guru.'

Love and God was never completed the way Asif intended, and an astounding number of people associated with this movie, including Guru Dutt, K. Asif, Sanjeev Kumar, Jayant, Nazir Hussain, Hiralal, Samson, Polson and Amar, passed away before the movie could be released, thereby giving it the dubious honour of being one of the most cursed movies of all times.

Asif's wife, Akhtar, released *Love and God* on 6 June 1986, dedicating it to the memory of those departed. The editing was highly compromised and several important scenes, including the climax, were omitted because they weren't shot by Asif. But the film, resplendent in its Technicolor, lavish period costumes and opulent sets designed meticulously by perfectionists, is an exemplary portrayal of mankind's indefatigable attempt at achieving a forever lost paradise.

10

Ways of the Heart

In the 1970s, one magazine claimed that Sanjeev Kumar was quite the flirt and loved the company of women. His name was associated with scores of actresses. He was linked to, among others, Nita Mehta, Jayshree T., Sulakshana Pandit and Shabana Azmi. Jayshree T. herself rubbishes these rumours, saying:

> I was too young for him! How could I have thought about marrying him? He was my guru, guide and philosopher. Do you know an English magazine had written nasty things about Sanjeev and me? I was really upset. I spoke to my cousin, Pramod Navalkar, then leader of the Shiv Sena, regarding this. Navalkar called the magazine's editor and said, 'I am Pramod Navalkar speaking and whatever you wrote in your magazine about my sister Jayshree, you have to clarify in your next issue. Otherwise, get ready to face the consequences.' In the very next issue, they apologized, and that was the end of the gossip.

After the completion of his debut film *Andaz* (1971), director Ramesh Sippy was looking for a subject for his next venture. He had a good team of writers—Salim Khan and Javed Akhtar—and they were in search of a fresh script to work on. Coincidentally, producer–director Pramod Chakravorty happened to be planning to make a new version of the superhit film *Ram Aur Shyam* (1967), focusing on identical female twins. The Dilip Kumar-starrer, in its turn, had been based on the English film *The Corsican Brothers* (1941). Chakravorty passed the idea on to his writer, Sachin Bhowmick, but, while the idea was still germinating, he heard that Ramesh Sippy was planning to make a film along the same lines. Thankfully, his film had not hit the floor yet, and he decided to put it on hold. According to Chakravorty, Sippy had somehow gotten hold of his idea and immediately told his writing team to develop a script around it. Unsurprisingly, both Chakravorty and Sippy envisioned the star of the time, Hema Malini, in the lead role.

Salim Khan considered casting Rajesh Khanna in this film since he was a superstar and his presence could yield results at the box office. He narrated the script to Rajesh Khanna without Sippy's knowledge. Rajesh Khanna, known to nurse a fragile ego and at the pinnacle of his career, wasn't prepared to be anything but the main lead. He told Salim Khan that he would consider the film only if Sippy changed the script to focus on identical male twins.

Ramesh Sippy enlisted Gulzar to write the dialogues as soon as *Andaz* released in 1971, but Gulzar had just got his first break as a director with *Mere Apne* (1971). Salim–Javed offered their services instead.

Seeta Aur Geeta is the story of twin sisters, Seeta and Geeta, who are separated at birth. Seeta is brought up by her uncle and aunt, who mistreat her and deprive her of her inheritance, and Geeta is raised by her slum-dwelling maternal aunt, who had stolen her from her cradle, and gets by working as a street performer. Seeta is homely, naive and submissive, while Geeta is vivacious, loud and street-smart. The plot turns into a comedy of errors where both are mistaken for each other. Amid all this, the sisters find love.

When Ramesh Sippy narrated the script to Hema Malini, she was not convinced that she could do justice to a role similar to what had been done by the legendary Dilip Kumar. Mindful of the divide between male and female stars in the industry, Sippy assured her that the audience would never compare her acting prowess to his. The only obstacle that remained was finding actors to play the twins' love interests, and this was solved when Dharmendra and Sanjeev Kumar agreed to play the parts. Although they were both stars in their own right, they had fewer, albeit powerful, scenes in the film.

Sanjeev agreed to do this film for only Rs 80,000. However, his role lacked depth and he couldn't find enough scope to showcase his talent. Javed Akhtar agrees, saying that the writers had only focused on the title roles. When Sanjeev approached the writers, they added shades of comedy to his role, enhancing the film immensely. Even in the climax, during the fight scenes, Sanjeev would chip in with his impeccable comic timing.

In one interview, Sanjeev Kumar spoke about his reasons for choosing to work in *Seeta Aur Geeta*. He had not even asked Sippy to narrate the script to him since he already knew that the film would focus on the heroine. He did the movie for the money, but that was not the sole reason. To him, the role had always been more important than the amount of screen time he received:

> You cannot say Dharam-ji and I were not an important part of *Seeta Aur Geeta*. Length-wise our roles were small, but they were crucial to the story. Can you imagine *Seeta Aur Geeta* without the two of us?

Although the Indo–Pak war of 1971 caused some setbacks, the film was completed in eighteen months and released on Diwali in 1972. A complete entertainment package, the movie was a phenomenal hit.

Sanjeev Kumar and Hema Malini became acquainted with each other while shooting for the song 'Hawa Ke Saath Saath', in which they had to skate through the picturesque roads of Mahabaleshwar. Since both actors were novice skaters, they fell an umpteen number of times. Ramesh Sippy, however, kept all the shots where they tripped, adding them to the song sequence to make it look natural. Eventually, a contraption in the form of a low trolley supported by sticks was devised to make it seem like they were whizzing through the valley. A makeshift arrangement, this was ill-equipped for the rough Indian roads. In one terrifying moment, the trolley came loose while both Hema Malini and Sanjeev Kumar were on it, and veered towards a cliff. Luckily the road bent inwards and both the actors fell away from the treacherous precipice. They escaped with minor cuts and bruises. This brush with death brought them closer. The moment they recovered from the accident, they were more concerned about each other than their own well-being. Many believe that this was the moment they began developing feelings for each other.

In love once again, Sanjeev was determined to marry Hema. Once again, he faced resistance from his mother. Mahesh Desai knew why: Shantaben did not want an actress as a daughter-in-law. Her rejection disheartened Hema enormously. Belonging to a tight-knit family, she could not imagine tying the knot without the whole-hearted approval of both their families. Sanjeev consoled her, telling her that Shantaben would come around to the union eventually. True to his word, Hema won Shantaben's heart. A humble woman despite her immense success, Hema always covered her head with her *pallu* and touched Shantaben's feet every time they met. She gradually became one of the Jariwala household.

Tarla Mehta fondly remembers the closeness between Sanjeev and Hema. Members of the same peer group at work, the two seemed destined to be together. On her birthday, Hema called Shantaben from Madras and said,

Mataji aaj mera janamdin hai—aap mujhe aashirwaad deejiye.
(Mother, it's my birthday today, please grant me your blessings.)

They ended up speaking on the phone for hours. Gayatri Patel says Hema held immense respect for Shantaben and the Jariwalas:

Whenever she went abroad, she brought something for my mom.

Whenever they visited Madras, she took great care of the family. Contrary to all expectations, Hema Malini became the only actress Shantaben was ready to accept as her daughter-in-law.

Expressive in front of the camera, in real life Sanjeev was awkward and shy. This lack of communication caused misunderstandings between the pair. Gayatri remembers one such occasion when there was some friction between the lovers. Although Sanjeev refused to talk about it, his sister could tell that something was amiss. He was not speaking to Hema. When Gayatri and her husband were leaving to attend Hema's dance show, Sanjeev refused to accompany them. After the show, a distressed Hema called Gayatri to ask what was wrong because she had no clue as to why Sanjeev was not speaking to her. She appealed to Gayatri to intervene, but his sister was helpless too, because Sanjeev would not discuss his relationship with her.

During this time, Hema was working with Dharmendra and the audience seemed to love this star pair's onscreen chemistry. Hema and Dharmendra worked together in many superhit movies, like *Sharafat* (1970), *Tum Haseen Main Jawan* (1970), *Naya Zamana* (1971), *Raja Jani* (1972) and *Jugnu* (1973), and everyone seemed to be certain that they were romantically involved in real life as well.

Meanwhile, Sanjeev was working with Leena Chandavarkar in *Anhonee* (1973), *Apne Rang Hazaar* (1975) and *Manchali* (1973) amid rumours about their alleged affair. Leena Chandavarkar laughs off those baseless rumours, saying:

One person my son Amit reminds me a lot of is Sanjeev Kumar. We shared a wonderful bond. He was always pulling my leg when we had a romantic scene to do. He would say, 'Oh, if only I were doing this scene with Hema Malini, how much I would have enjoyed it.' I would retort, 'Dream away, dream boy. I too wish Dharmendra was here instead of you.' This banter would go on before the entire unit, to their endless amusement. Sometimes, he would come to the set and say, 'I don't believe this, you are actually looking beautiful today, touch wood,' and touch my head.

Eventually, the Jariwalas decided to visit Hema's family in Madras and ask for her hand. Sanjeev, Hema and Shantaben planned the visit, fixed a date and got their tickets. As was customary, Shantaben arrived at Hema's home with boxes of sweets, and Hema Malini's mother, Jaya Chakravarthy, was happy to meet Sanjeev's family. The cultural differences did not pose a hurdle, but Hema Malini's film career became a bone of contention. As Hema Malini told veteran journalist Bhawana Somaaya later,

> My mother's ambition was to give me all that she couldn't have for herself. In her case, giving did not include small worldly comforts but big dreams, big aspirations. She had wanted to be a dancer, but couldn't. She learnt music, though reared in an orthodox Iyengar family. Making me an artiste was like bhakti or tapasya for her.

Firm in her ambitions for her daughter, Jaya Chakravarthy declared to Shantaben,

> It is my pleasure that you have agreed to accept my daughter Hema as your daughter-in-law. But my only condition is that she continue her career as an actress after her marriage.

For the Jariwala family this was a difficult condition to accept. Shantaben and Sanjeev were clear from the start that they would not allow Hema to act in films after marriage. According to Gayatri Patel, Hema herself had promised Sanjeev that she would complete only her pending assignments before bidding farewell to the film world.

Hema, however, could not withstand her mother's iron will. She was one of the highest-paid actresses of her time; she could understand the reason behind her mother's decision. Hema was hopeful that Sanjeev would eventually come around and allow her to carry on with her career. Sanjeev remained hopeful that Hema would convince her mother, and he stayed in touch with her.

It became increasingly difficult for Sanjeev to understand Hema. Trapped between her mother and Sanjeev, she wavered irresolutely, going this way one day and the other, the next. She asked Sanjeev to let her continue with her acting career for a while. As soon as the film-makers heard of their marriage, they would stop casting her, and she would be able to settle down at home with him and his family. But Sanjeev was not ready to compromise.

Rajesh Khanna knew about Hema and Sanjeev's differences. When Damu Jhaveri, the general secretary of INT, organized a premiere show for a Hollywood film at Sterling Cinema, Bombay, as a fundraiser, both Rajesh Khanna and Sanjeev Kumar were invited. INT producer Bachoo Sampat recalls the organizers asking Rajesh to bring Sharmila Tagore with him, since they were shooting together, and asking Sanjeev Kumar to bring Hema Malini.

Both agreed to attend the premiere. Rajesh Khanna knew that Sanjeev was invited, but Sanjeev did not know that Rajesh Khanna was coming. Sanjeev arrived early, and, at the request of the announcer, straightaway sat in his designated chair on the stage. Well-known personalities like Mahesh Desai, Tarla Joshi, Tarla Mehta, Kalpana Diwan, Bachoo Sampat, Pravin Joshi and Padmarani had graced the occasion. No sooner had everyone settled down than suddenly, heads whipped around and hushed whispers rippled across the auditorium.

Sanjeev looked up to see what the commotion was about and was shocked to see Rajesh Khanna walking down the carpeted aisle holding hands with Hema Malini. Both of them walked to the front row of the cinema hall and sat down as part of the audience.

Sanjeev was humiliated and hurt. Hema was equally shocked to see him. She had merely accompanied Rajesh Khanna at his insistence and did not know of the animosity that existed between the two. Although she could gauge to some extent the damage she had unwittingly inflicted, she did not dare confront Rajesh Khanna. Sanjeev Kumar stepped down from the stage and joined the audience in a different row, far away from them. None of them spoke to each other during the show.

Many members of the audience were shocked by Rajesh Khanna's disrespectful behaviour. Tarla Mehta felt terrible for her friend, while Nargis Irani, Aspi Irani's sister, admired how Sanjeev kept his cool. His relationship with Hema was already hanging by a thread and seeing her with Rajesh Khanna in public would prove to be the last straw.

Sanjeev's friends tried to explain to him that Rajesh Khanna had done it on purpose to humiliate him and that Hema was innocent. But Sanjeev took this insult to heart. He spent a sleepless night nursing a troubled mind and grieving heart.

The next morning, he was to shoot for Raghunath Jhalani's film *Anamika* with Jaya Bhaduri at S.D. Burman's bungalow Sur Mandir, Khar, Bombay. The song 'Baahon Mein Chale Aao' was being filmed. Sanjeev delivered every shot perfectly, but as soon as each shot was done, his face darkened. It was plain to all that he was trying to stem the flow of tears. Jaya Bhaduri could sense her co-star was upset. Later, in one of her interviews, she mused on that day, saying she tried to make him laugh but failed, and he tried to distract himself but could not. At last, during the lunch break, he told her what had happened. She was shocked. How had he been working all day in such emotional turmoil? After their lunch, even Jaya Bhaduri could not perform, so moved was she by his troubles. He told her to set it aside. As artistes, their first duty was to perform their given character, and the audience had nothing to do with their personal lives. It was the first glimpse she had into his dedication to his work.

Sanjeev was avoiding Hema Malini's calls, but she was not easily deterred. She went to Parin Villa to speak to him directly. Sanjeev was sitting with Jamnadas. They had a row about their career, marriage and the Rajesh Khanna incident then and there. After going round in circles, when he asked her for a definitive answer about her intention to work in films after marriage, she said that she wasn't ready to give it up. He asked her to leave him forever, and then walked out of the room. Hema couldn't believe that this was the end, just like that. She sat there stupefied, and, when it finally dawned on her that there was nothing more to be done, she left as well. Rehana Sultan recalls ruefully:

And so they both parted ways. More than friends, Sanjeev needed
a wife who could take care of him, and Hema was capable of that.

Actress Sulakshana Pandit, who had worked with Sanjeev Kumar in *Uljhan* and *Waqt ki Deewar*, was in love with him. After his break-up with Hema Malini, a lot had been written about Sulakshana and Sanjeev, but it was merely an unrequited love affair. By her own admission, Sulakshana Pandit once went to a Hanuman temple with him and asked him to put sindoor in her *maang*. He refused to do so, saying he was still in love with Hema Malini and had made up his mind to not marry at all.

After parting ways with Hema Malini, Sanjeev learnt that his friend Jeetendra had proposed to her. He felt betrayed but didn't say a word to Jeetendra when he worked with him in *Swarag Narak* (1978), *Jaani Dushman* (1979), *Takkar* (1980) and *Waqt Ki Deewar* (1980), to name a few. He even played a guest role in Jeetendra's home production *Jyoti Bane Jwala* (1980).

So far as Hema was concerned, Sanjeev decided never to work with her again. In two of his films, *Sholay* and *Trishul*, Hema was playing important roles, but even in the same frame they never exchanged any dialogue with each other. This also became the reason for Sanjeev Kumar's turning down Sippy's *Shaan*, where he was offered the role of the heartless villain Shakaal. The moment he came to know that Hema Malini was supposed to be a part of the movie (she was signed on for the character that Bindiya Goswami eventually played), he refused the role, and it eventually went to Kulbhushan Kharbanda, who made the character Shakaal memorable in his own uniquely terrifying way.

Hema Malini always avoided talking about Sanjeev Kumar in her interviews, but, on one occasion, she expressed her displeasure at journalists' probing into her personal affairs. Like Sanjeev Kumar, Hema maintained that while love was important, it had its place, and it could not interfere with work. In an interview with Bhawana Somaaya for *Junior G*'s April 1991 issue, Hema broke her silence:

> A Sanjeev Kumar who desired a stay-at-home, all-sacrificing wife who would care for his ageing mother and support him, while he mesmerized the audience and won accolades, seems like a caricature of a male chauvinist. But before judging him too harshly, let's consider the era we are dealing with. Back in the day, it was common to look down upon women who chose to be a part of showbiz. A 'good woman' and a 'good wife' was a woman who chose her family over herself and her career, a tireless homemaker who helped her husband reach the pinnacle of success—rubbed oil in her mother-in-law's hair, taught her daughter good manners and helped her son with his homework. Times have changed and women are liberated from this unfair burden. The truth is that an 'ideal woman' or, for that matter, an 'ideal man' is a myth, and perhaps this is the reason Sanjeev Kumar could not settle down in his lifetime. The perfectionist in him searched for the perfect woman—who frankly doesn't exist.

According to Sarika, after an age, her

'Hari Uncle' just wanted to enjoy his life in his own way.

Eating and drinking with his friends after work, his life seemed perfect, and he did not want it to change. His carefree and colourful lifestyle would not sit well with any woman. Marriage might have put a stop to his evening revelries, and he decided to stay away from such a demanding commitment, especially after his second heart attack. One wonders what his life would have been like if he had married a woman he loved. Would he have been more careful with his health? Would children have made him more mindful of his precious life?

11

A Versatile Actor

In the 1970s, films had become monotonously formulaic. Producers feared to even venture a step in another direction for the risk of losing money. Even if the producers gave their consent to an unusual storyline, film financiers and distributers would insist on including Mehmood for comic relief or adding a song sequence shot in the picturesque valleys of Kashmir, all in a bid to play it safe and not stray too far from what they believed the audience expected.

Due to this, stars in the '70s came up with their 'trademark' styles, and star pairs were in huge demand. 'Once successful, always successful' was the mantra of the film industry. Jeetendra wore white shoes and frequently broke into jaunty dance steps, earning him the moniker 'Jumping Jack'; Rajesh Khanna tilted his head to one side and nodded on cue; Shatrughan Sinha thundered '*Khamosh!*' to warn his adversaries; and Amitabh Bachchan portrayed the 'angry young man' in film after film after film. Shammi Kapoor, Biswajeet, Dharmendra, Shashi Kapoor, among many others, were forced to play repetitive roles.

Sanjeev Kumar, however, went against the tide, essaying diverse and complex roles, each starkly different from the other. There was no pinning him down to one stereotype. He knew that audiences were capricious and stereotypes ran the risk of becoming stale. His love for the craft and penchant to experiment made him pick films solely for the thrill of challenging himself.

Bimal Roy's son-in-law, Basu Bhattacharya, had just won a National Award for Best Feature Film with *Teesri Kasam* (1966), but the film had bombed at the box office. Consequently, he couldn't find a producer willing to invest in his new venture. He approached the Film Finance Corporation (FFC), now known as the National Film Development Corporation (NFDC). The NFDC approved the film, but it had to be completed on a shoestring budget. Cinematographer Nandu Bhattacharya, music composer Kanu Roy, lyricist Gulzar and actors Sanjeev Kumar and Tanuja were all willing to work for little or no pay. Sagar Sarhadi, one of Basu Bhattacharya's old theatre acquaintances, had been roped in to write the dialogues for the film. Pran had been slated to play the male lead, but he backed out when he felt that his performance left much to be desired. Sanjeev, who was asked by Sarhadi to replace Pran, agreed to it without hesitation. This was a surprising choice for most stars of the time. According to veteran actor Sulbha Arya:

> Sanjeev was an actor who worked for all. He never believed in the distinction between A- and B-grade films. Some films he signed for money, some for friends and some for good roles. Whenever he got challenging roles, he worked as hard as he could even if he had to compromise on his price.

Sanjeev Kumar agreed to an amount less than his market price, which ran into lakhs, for Basu Bhattacharya's film, a gesture he repeated when working with internationally renowned director Satyajit Ray.

Anubhav (1971) dealt with a refreshing subject. Amar and Meeta Sen are a childless couple who've been married for several years. Amar is busy and has no time for his wife. Trouble arrives in the form of Shashi Bhushan, Meeta's ex-flame, as his unexpected return causes strife in the marriage.

With no money to spare for elaborate sets or expensive studios, both Sanjeev and Tanuja opened their doors to Basu Bhattacharya to shoot at their homes. Tanuja's flat in Usha Kiran Apartments, Haji Ali, was bigger than Sanjeev's Parin Villa, so most of the film was shot in her flat. With a reputation for arriving late to set, and now with the added travel to Tanuja's, some distance from Pali Hill, Sanjeev would reach the location at almost two in the afternoon. Late though he was, he was never in a hurry to leave. The set itself was a fun place, and all the members of the crew had a roaring time. Caught between too many Bengalis—Basu Bhattacharya, Kapil Kumar, Manik Chatterjee, Nandu Bhattacharya and Tanuja—poor Sanjeev would often feel left out. He held his own, however. Basu Bhattacharya remembers him as a naughty man; he found Sanjeev's company immensely enjoyable and admired his humility. Even after achieving the heights of stardom, Sanjeev remained a soft-spoken, respectful man who could easily mould himself into any given character. *Anubhav* was a success, winning a National Film Award for Second-Best Feature Film. It is still remembered for the songs, voiced by Geeta Dutt, which gained even more of a haunting quality by the fact that this would be the last film she sang for. She passed away in 1972 of liver cirrhosis. Following the success of the film, Basu Bhattacharya completed a trilogy on marital discord with *Aavishkar* (1973) and *Griha Pravesh* (1979). He cast Sanjeev Kumar again for *Griha Pravesh*, but *Aavishkar* went to his rival, Rajesh Khanna.

Setting personal differences aside, Sanjeev helped Jeetendra, at a time when the latter was looking to get away from his Jumping Jack image, advising him to take up diverse roles, perhaps with Gulzar. *Parichay* (1972), a film based on the Bengali novel *Rangeen Uttarain* by Raj Kumar Maitra, proved a landmark in Jeetendra's career. Gulzar also cast Sanjeev Kumar as Jaya Bhaduri's father, much to Jeetendra's shock, because the duo was almost simultaneously playing husband and wife in Gulzar's *Koshish* (1972). He had no cause for fear, though. Jaya was close to both Gulzar and Sanjeev, and together, the three created magic on screen.

Jeetendra took some time to find his footing. His friends discouraged him throughout the making of the movie because they believed he was harming his image. Sanjeev Kumar supported him and asked him to put complete faith in Gulzar. True to his word, the film, when it released, had all the qualities of a timeless classic. Kishore Kumar's song 'Musafir Hoon Yaaron' would go on to be one of the most successful film songs of all time.

Parichay was very well received by the audience. It changed Jeetendra's image and entertained everyone with a storyline full of innocence, mischief and tenderness. Lata Mangeshkar would win the National Film Award for Best Female Playback Singer for 'Biti Na Bitaayee Raina', a song Jeetendra had nearly voted out of the film.

12

A Legendary Rivalry

The film industry is famously riddled with jealousy and fierce rivalries, defined by hierarchies. Stars tend to be fussy about seemingly trivial issues, such as whose name appears first during credit roll, who gets a better make-up room and whose costumes and shot angles are better. One such rivalry was the one between Sanjeev Kumar and Rajesh Khanna.

Gautam Chintamani recalls (in the book *The Loneliness of Being Rajesh Khanna*) that Rajesh Khanna (then called Jatin), despite being a struggling actor, would go to auditions in the latest sports cars and enjoy a monthly allowance of Rs 1000. However, Rajesh Khanna had his share of hurdles: rivals like Sanjeev Kumar often scored over him due to associations with the influential IPTA, taking away contracts that were almost within his grasp.

While both Sanjeev and Rajesh hailed from the INT, it was the language that had separated them. Sanjeev mainly performed in Gujarati plays, while Kaka performed in Hindi. Due to the paucity of Gujarati theatre artists of Sanjeev's calibre in Bombay, directors were eager to work with him. Rajesh Khanna, on the other hand, was one of many Hindi-speaking actors desperate for a break. At one time, while Sanjeev was acting in five different plays simultaneously,

Rajesh barely had one. Reduced to playing small roles, like that of a doorman in V.K. Sharma's *Mere Desh Ke Gaon*, Kaka had watched from the sidelines as Sanjeev walked away with meatier roles and awards. It took numerous attempts for Rajesh Khanna to finally lay his hands on a college festival award for his role in *Aur Diya Bujh Jaye*. When he won this award, he organized a party to celebrate, and invited Sanjeev Kumar. The latter did not bother to even respond to the invitation, let alone show up.

Notably, although Sanjeev received offers for film roles before Rajesh Khanna did, he had also been struggling for longer. It had taken Sanjeev five years to make the move from theatre to cinema, while Kaka was on stage for barely two years before shifting to the silver screen, according to the director Ramesh Talwar.

Perhaps the two came from worlds so far apart that they could never reconcile their differences. A dishevelled Hari in his ragged kurta pyjamas might have seemed to Rajesh Khanna the very antithesis to the glamorous world of cinema they both were aspiring to enter. Rajesh Khanna, meanwhile, flitting between auditions in his expensive car, would have presented the picture of privilege to the struggling Sanjeev Kumar.

While still a stage actor, Rajesh Khanna was a reticent man, only interacting with his fellow actor Anju Mahendru. He would come to meet her while she was working in B.S. Thapa's *Mehenga Sauda*, but remained aloof from all the other actors present on set, including Sanjeev Kumar. Many assumed that his attitude implied an arrogant belief that he was made for bigger, better things than the Hindi stage.

Anju Mahendru, meanwhile, was good friends with Sanjeev Kumar as well. Rajesh Khanna was often suspicious of their friendship, their easy camaraderie making him believe that they shared a romantic relationship. Although Anju tried to convince him of the contrary, he continued to harbour his suspicions. Sanjeev Kumar had often warned Anju to steer clear of Rajesh Khanna, clearly a man given to jealous fits of passion. He did not believe it would be possible for her to find a stable life with such a fickle man.

In 1969, setting personal differences aside, Rajesh Khanna and Sanjeev Kumar came together to work with G.P. Sippy for *Bandhan*. Anju Mahendru also acted in the film. Despite the friction, however, they behaved professionally and the movie was completed without any untoward incidents. As time passed, Rajesh Khanna delivered hit after hit, and soon came to be known as the first superstar of Hindi cinema. Sanjeev had made considerable strides as well and was offered roles in numerous critically acclaimed movies. Known for his sensitive, visceral portrayals, he came to play a variety of roles, while Rajesh Khanna carved a niche for himself in the romantic genre.

Towards the end of the 1960s, Hrishikesh Mukherjee had started planning his ambitious project *Anand* (1970) with N.C. Sippy. Based on Raj Kapoor and Hrishikesh Mukherjee's friendship, the film was initially slated to star Kishore Kumar and Mehmood. The title role would go to Kishore Kumar, while Mehmood would play Babu Moshai. Unfortunately, Hrishikesh Mukherjee and Kishore Kumar had a tiff and fell out. Consequently, Kishore left the film and Mehmood followed his friend, although he was unaware of what had transpired. In his biography *Mehmood: A Man of Many Moods*, Mehmood says:

> If I had known what had happened with Hrishi-da at that time, I would have spoken to Kishore and sorted the matter.

When Rajesh Khanna heard of *Anand*, he approached the director for the titular role. Delighted at the opportunity to cast the superstar, N.C. Sippy and Hrishikesh Mukherjee readily agreed.

The role of Babu Moshai was still available and Mukherjee decided to approach Sanjeev Kumar, who had already worked with him in *Satyakam* (1969) and *Aashirwad* (1968). Sanjeev, as always, spotted the potential of the script and agreed to do the film. Unfortunately, when Rajesh Khanna was informed of Sanjeev's casting, he grew insecure about his role. Although he had the titular role, the development of Babu Moshai's character was crucial to the plotline. Khanna did not want to share the limelight with Sanjeev. Ultimately, Amitabh Bachchan was cast in the role that Mukherjee had reserved for Sanjeev. This was the first of the two times that Sanjeev Kumar lost a role to Bachchan; the second being for Rajshri Productions' acclaimed project *Saudagar* (1973).

As Anju Mahendru remembers, Rajesh Khanna always remained insecure about his acting prowess in comparison to Sanjeev's. Every time she went to meet Sanjeev, Rajesh would get upset. Sagar Sarhadi remembers this as well. Almost everyone knew the two actors could not stand each other.

The writer duo Salim–Javed was very close to Rajesh Khanna, having written a screenplay for his film *Haathi Mere Saathi* (1971). Salim Khan and Rajesh Khanna would meet every day at Aashirwad, Khanna's Carter Road residence. On one occasion, when Salim met Rajesh, he was sitting on the bonnet of his car, holding a film magazine. He asked Khan if he had indeed hailed Sanjeev Kumar as one of the best actors of his time in an interview featured therein. A straightforward man, Salim replied that he had. Visibly upset, Rajesh Khanna asked him if he thought Sanjeev was the better actor. Taken aback, Salim Khan explained that his praise for Sanjeev Kumar had been in the context of a specific role, and if he was interviewed about Rajesh Khanna's role, he would have appropriate praise for him as well. Rajesh Khanna was not to be comforted. Brooding, he took off for another shoot, leaving Khan dumbfounded. The incident stayed with Salim Khan for a long time. Chintamani quotes him, saying that Kaka was extremely insecure and possessive. Later, when Salim–Javed started working with other actors, he took it as a betrayal of sorts. As Chintamani writes:

> By now, Khanna's insecurity had started taking a toll on him. As a person who by nature was highly insecure and continually sought positive reinforcement, he had surrounded himself with yes-men . . .

Since a palpable tension existed between Sanjeev and Rajesh, very few film-makers were keen on taking on the task of working with them together. However, J. Om Prakash made the surprising choice to cast them both in his directorial debut, *Aap Ki Kasam* (1974), a remake of the Malayalam film *Vazhve Mayam* (1970).

For the lead role, Rajesh Khanna was his first choice. He was a star who could pull huge crowds to the theatre, and following the success of *Anand*, audiences knew him as a capable actor as well. Having decided to cast him, Om Prakash made a small change to the script—an ending similar to that in *Anand*. Armed with his script, Om Prakash met Khanna and narrated the film to him. Aware of Om Prakash's impressive track record, Rajesh Khanna accepted the role eagerly. He was then informed that Sanjeev Kumar would be cast as the second lead. He seemed acquiescent, and Om Prakash went to meet Sanjeev Kumar.

By this time, Sanjeev had started playing lead roles in acclaimed films like *Khilona* (1970), and Om Prakash was worried he would not accept the role. Upon meeting Sanjeev Kumar, however, Om Prakash was impressed with his humility. Before he narrated the script to him, he warned him that he wanted to cast him in the second lead. Sanjeev agreed to the role. Om Prakash signed him on for two other films as well, *Aakraman* (1975) and *Aandhi* (1975). According to one of Kumar's friends, Sanjeev supposedly signed the film seeing it as an opportunity to sort out his differences with Khanna. Om Prakash was determined to complete his film on time.

He went through every detail with his technicians to ensure that the shoots ran smoothly and with minimal interruptions. The first shoot was held at Mehboob Studios. Prakash decided to begin shooting with the most crucial and tricky scene—where Rajesh Khanna was to slap Sanjeev Kumar. Om Prakash wanted to see whether the actors would be able to work together. Before he started the shoot, he warned the cast and crew that while he was open to suggestions, he would not tolerate interference or indiscipline on his sets. He explained the scene in detail to both actors together, then ordered the cameras to roll. The scene was shot without a hitch, and the actors shared the stage effortlessly. Although a first-time director, Om Prakash handled the shoot so well that Sanjeev Kumar later congratulated him for it.

Om Prakash remembered Sanjeev Kumar as a flawless actor—fluent in Hindi despite being Gujarati, with proper diction and dialogue delivery. The only problem with Kumar was his perpetual tardiness. Prakash got so used to Sanjeev being late that, to save time, he would complete scenes with other actors before Sanjeev arrived.

The climax of the film was shot with Rajesh Khanna's character dying in Sanjeev Kumar's lap. Khanna was sure he would walk away with the laurels for the scene as the dying hero, but Sanjeev's dialogues were so powerful that they stole the show. His screen presence, coupled with the haunting song 'Zindagi Ke Safar Mein' enchanted the audiences.

Aap Ki Kasam was completed in ten months and released within a year. It was a superhit at the box office, and Prakash worked with Khanna and Kumar again in *Aakraman*. Unfortunately, *Aakraman* did not do very well. Although Sanjeev claimed that he had no problem working with Khanna, putting his craft before petty rivalries, this was the last film in which they would work together. Long after this, Prakash worked with Sanjeev Kumar again for *Apnapan* (1977). His memories of the actor were summed up best, according to the film-maker himself, by the song 'Aadmi Musafir Hai'.

Over twenty-five years in the industry, Sanjeev Kumar and Rajesh Khanna never visited each other at their homes. However, in November 1985, when Sanjeev Kumar breathed his last, Rajesh Khanna visited to pay his respects, his eyes brimming with tears.

13

A New Day

Hindi cinema was changing once again, shifting away from clichés and towards cinematic flair and theatricality. Bollywood directors looked southwards for inspiration and discovered avant-garde ideas that challenged the existing notions of storytelling and offered a fresh perspective to cinemagoers.

The film *Navarathri* (1964), made in both Tamil and Telugu, captured the attention of Hindi film-makers. While several producers wanted to buy the rights for the film, they could not decide on an actor who could do justice to the script. When M.P. Ali bought the rights to the script, set to be titled *Naya Din Nayee Raat* (1974), he decided to convince Dilip Kumar to take on the task of playing the lead's nine different roles in the film. To make sure that the star would agree, he enlisted director A. Bhim's help. Ali was convinced that the film would be a game changer in Bollywood.

Much to Ali's dismay, Dilip Kumar turned down his offer. As his wife Sayeeda remembered, he spent the entire night tossing and turning and set off the next morning to appeal to Dilip Kumar again. According to cinematographer Sudarshan Nag, this time Dilip Kumar suggested Sanjeev's name in his stead.

Why did Dilip Kumar refuse such an opportunity? The great man himself said that he had always ensured never to repeat himself on screen. When Ali approached him, he was already playing triple roles in Mushir–Riaz's *Bairaag* (1976) and had previously played identical twins in *Ram Aur Shyam* (1967). Not keen on disappointing his fans with the same stale fare, he refused Ali's offer.

The role went to Sanjeev Kumar, and he began to prepare to play the nine roles the script demanded. He refrained from watching the other renditions, afraid to influence his interpretation of the roles. However, he was an admirer of Akkineni Nageswara Rao, the actor who acted in the Telugu film. When he met Rao in Madras, he told him he was playing the roles and asked for his blessings. Meanwhile, despite the script being heavily biased towards the male actor, Jaya Bhaduri agreed to do the film. The shooting started soon after.

The film presented Sanjeev with unique challenges. For one of the scenes, he played a circus trainer surrounded by lions and tigers. Although due precautions were taken to ensure his safety, the lion would roar every time Sanjeev approached, and the actor would hesitate and retreat. The one-take actor ended up doing eight retakes for this shot alone. It took a year and a half for the shooting to be completed.

When *Naya Din Nayee Raat* was about to be released, Sanjeev was desperate to know how the audience would receive it. Prior to the release, a special screening was arranged for Dilip Kumar, and the veteran actor was deeply impressed with Sanjeev Kumar's performance. The film, when released for public viewing, was preceded by a voiceover by Dilip Kumar, praising Sanjeev Kumar's astonishing skills as an actor.

The immense success of the film made Sanjeev Kumar the toast of tinsel town once more. Nageswara Rao called Sanjeev to congratulate him on his phenomenal performance. Sanjeev's friend, Deven Verma, however, noticed a small slip he had made in the film—keeping his shoulder raised during one scene, a trait he had honed to fit another character in the same film. Sanjeev was flattered and also taken aback that Verma had paid such close attention to his work. When Shabana Azmi criticized his performance on a few salient points, he listened quietly, without interruption, then, when she left, he remarked:

> Today she taught me how to act. Perhaps tomorrow she will teach Dilip Kumar too.

14

Meeting Suchitra Sen

J. Om Prakash, for his third film with Sanjeev Kumar, handed over directorial responsibilities to Gulzar and appointed writer Sachin Bhowmick to work on the story. He intended to create a script that would rope in Suchitra Sen, one of the finest actresses of Bengal.

In an interview with Saba Bashir mentioned in the book *Gulzar's Aandhi: Insights into the Film*, Gulzar remembers Om Prakash calling him to direct a thriller to be set in a hospital, featuring Suchitra Sen and Sanjeev Kumar. The story had been written by Sachin Bhowmick keeping the two actors in mind. In a meeting with Om Prakash, Sanjeev Kumar and Sachin Bhowmick, Gulzar said that he didn't particularly like the story. It seemed to be a run-of-the-mill Bambaiya story, not worth calling Suchitra Sen to Bombay for. Bhowmick agreed.

Gulzar told the others what he had in mind: two characters' romantic relationship, their separation and the woman's subsequent engagement in politics. At the time, films on politicians were few and far between, and cinemagoers had not seen the inner workings of nationwide politics on the screen. Om Prakash liked the story idea and asked Gulzar to write it. The film-maker–writer penned the synopsis in around two weeks and presented it to Om Prakash.

Having finalized the script, Om Prakash travelled to Kolkata, and Suchitra Sen readily agreed to play the role. Her standing in the industry was such that most sources claim she was paid more than Sanjeev Kumar for her role in the film.

Sanjeev was so excited to work with Sen that he developed cold feet when the shoot finally began. Intimidated by her calibre, discipline and flawless reputation, he feared that she would take issue with his habit of arriving late to the sets. He was also well acquainted with the disagreement Sen had had with the director Raj Khosla on the sets of *Bambai Ka Babu* (1960), when she had dragged him to court for disturbing her night's sleep. The crew of *Bambai Ka Babu* had gathered at a hotel to celebrate a colleague's birthday. Coincidentally, they chose the same hotel where Sen was putting up with her husband. Loud music and boisterous conversation blared from the party room, disturbing Sen and her husband. The couple couldn't sleep a wink and Sen complained to the hotel manager. The manager was unwilling to offend his high-profile guests, so Sen barged into the room with her husband to confront the revellers herself. She found Khosla among the guests and reprimanded him harshly. Khosla took umbrage, unceremoniously asking Sen to leave. Sen packed up and left for Kolkata the following day, causing the shooting to get cancelled.

Many did their best to patch things up between the actress and the director, but neither would budge. Things took a turn for the worse when Sen filed a case against Khosla for not clearing her pending fee and Khosla retaliated by filing a counter-complaint at the Producers' Association against Sen for leaving the project incomplete. The judgment passed was in Khosla's favour and Sen was asked to complete the movie before claiming her due amount. Sen complied and the movie was completed.

Wary of her infamous temper, Sanjeev was always careful around Suchitra Sen. The film was shot in Srinagar, and belying all expectations, Kumar was never late. Suchitra Sen commanded such respect that she was addressed as 'Sir' by everyone, including

Gulzar. As the film proceeded, Sanjeev began to feel her centrality to the movie more and more deeply. He came to believe that the film would be remembered for her seminal work only. However, he kept his doubts to himself and finished the shooting.

The movie had a scene where A.K. Hangal, who was playing the role of their domestic help, had to pick up Sanjeev's coat and help him put it on. Sanjeev objected to this scene as disrespectful towards Hangal, who was not only his senior but also one of his earliest mentors. Hangal took Sanjeev aside and explained to him that they must put aside their real-life identities before the camera and become whoever the script demanded them to be. He also reminded Sanjeev that before he joined the film industry, he had been a tailor by profession and had helped many people put on coats on a regular basis. Sanjeev agreed to do the scene. However, Gulzar removed it on the editing table.

A day after its release, veteran actor Ashok Kumar called Sanjeev and told him that Suchitra Sen was stunning, as usual, but Sanjeev had fared even better. Delighted, Sanjeev made Ashok Kumar repeat himself so he could savour the praise.

Much has been written about Suchitra Sen's remarkable performance in the film. Maitreyee B. Chowdhury points out that *Aandhi* brought Suchitra Sen the national adulation she had always desired. The evolution of her character from a spirited woman in love to an influential politician and ultimately a world-weary woman demonstrated her incredible skill as an actor.

Aandhi also courted controversy given the belief that Suchitra Sen's Aarti Devi was based on Indira Gandhi, then prime minister of India. While Indira Gandhi's appearance and mannerisms were used as references, Gulzar claimed that the plot had nothing to do with her experiences. Many took offence at the fact that Aarti Devi was shown imbibing alcohol on screen. Unfortunately, the film was released during the Emergency and was banned after running for only twenty weeks in the theatres. Although Prakash initially received praise for the film and even a letter from the government congratulating him on the film's selection for the Moscow Film Festival, the screening itself was cancelled. Sanjeev Kumar was with J. Om Prakash in Moscow, and they returned home greatly disappointed. The film had already been running for weeks, so the film-makers decided to modify two scenes. Even so, the screening of *Aandhi* was stopped in violation of existing censor protocols.

A.K. Hangal remembers Sanjeev Kumar's chagrin about the government's decision. The film had been a success while it ran, and now it seemed that one of his stellar performances would be consigned to the archives forever. The information and broadcasting minister at the time, Vidya Charan Shukla, a friend of Om Prakash, told the producer to approach the prime minister for help. Meanwhile, Gulzar and Sanjeev Kumar were advised to keep mum in public regarding the film.

Om Prakash wrote a short letter to Indira Gandhi, informing her that he had been adversely affected by the Emergency. He received a call from the PMO in three days telling him that he had been permitted a fifteen-minute audience with Mrs Gandhi.

Over the course of the conversation, Om Prakash realized that Mrs Gandhi had not even seen the film! He confessed to her that while the appearance of the leading lady was inspired by her style, he felt that it did not warrant the film being banned. Assuring him that she would do the needful, Indira Gandhi concluded the meeting. The following day, Om Prakash was informed by Vidya Charan Shukla that the film had been cleared for screening.

Nevertheless, the process took another six months to go through. The film had to be screened by the censor board once again, and the scenes with the leading lady smoking and drinking were cut. However, on its second release, the film did not draw audiences as it had done before.

Despite the roadblocks, *Aandhi* remains one of Sanjeev Kumar's landmark films. Gulzar says:

Sanjeev was born to act; he played all his roles with conviction.

Despite wearing the same costume for *Aandhi* and *Mausam* (1975), he portrayed completely different characters on screen in the two movies. According to Sarika, however, his acting was secondary to Sen's in the film. His performance, in her opinion, was far superior in a film like *Anamika* (1973).

Aandhi was Suchitra Sen's last film in Hindi. Sanjeev Kumar and Suchitra Sen never appeared on screen together again, but they remained lifelong friends.

15

The Landmark Films

Koshish (1972): The Crowning Glory

Our Hindi film industry has been amply blessed with mavericks who dare to tread the road less travelled. Gulzar is one such visionary. When the Hindi film industry was inundated with romantic melodramas and action potboilers that displayed a staggering lack of imagination, Gulzar was undertaking a journey to break this spell of monotony and give the audience a jolt of something absolutely original.

Unfortunately, an intellectual breakthrough is not enough without steady monetary support to ensure that these ideas get to see the light of day. Gulzar had already been turned down by two famous producers when he narrated a story to his friend Sippy. Sippy listened with rapt attention to the story of a disabled couple who could neither hear nor speak. He was taken by the originality of the idea, realizing that it would be a challenge to explore the tale on celluloid. Not only did it have the markings of a classic, but it was set to be made by the notorious perfectionist himself. Written with Sanjeev Kumar in mind as the lead actor, the protagonist of the film *Koshish* was named Haricharan Mathur, a name bearing a close resemblance to

Sanjeev's own. The story of an extraordinary couple born with physical impairments and their triumphant love and resilience, *Koshish* would star Jaya Bhaduri as Aarti to Sanjeev's Haricharan.

Both Sippy and Gulzar were convinced that Sanjeev was the man for the role. The former had been impressed with his formidable talent during the shooting of *Aashirwad* (1968), but it was Sanjeev himself who came to harbour some doubts. Troubled by the challenge this character would pose, he could not be sure that he would excel at portraying nuances on screen with no dialogues to support him. His previous experience playing a differently abled character in *Khilona* had not prepared him enough for this experience. He decided to place complete faith in Gulzar, however, recognizing that this script could well prove to be a landmark film in the history of Indian cinema. Dedicated to the demand for verisimilitude on screen, Tarla Joshi remembers Sanjeev Kumar going to two institutions for the deaf and mute in Worli and Dadar in order to prepare for his role.

Apart from his research for the role, Sanjeev also drew inspiration from his memories of his aunt Daiben, who suffered from the same impairments and used sign language to communicate. Soon, he had struck on the method he would adopt: as he always told his friend Tarla, the true mark of an actor lay in his ability to communicate with the audience through merely his eyes. Armed with his research and the introspection that accompanied it, Sanjeev was ready to work on the film for a paltry sum of Rs 60,000. Entirely committed to the project, he turned down an offer from the great Sagar Sarhadi because the dates would clash with *Koshish*.

While the lead actor fell into place easily, the actress opposite him was a different matter altogether. The obvious pick for the role was Moushumi Chatterjee, who had earned accolades with her portrayal of a visually challenged woman in *Anuraag* (1972), her Hindi film debut. Both Gulzar and Sippy were of the opinion that she could play Aarti with considerable élan. When they approached Moushumi with the offer, she readily accepted. Shooting was slated to be completed within four months on a limited budget.

N.C. Sippy's son, Raj N. Sippy, joined Gulzar as the assistant director, and the set of a house was made at Mohan Studios, Andheri East. As soon as shooting began, however, Gulzar noticed an odd daily trend. Before he could wrap up the day's session and announce pack-up, Moushumi Chatterjee would ask him permission to allow her to leave as early as six in the evening. Raj N. Sippy attests that the agreement they had arrived at previously was clear. They were to shoot from nine in the morning to eight in the evening, but the leading lady's need to leave the set early threw a spanner in the works.

Gulzar was a man of principle, very disciplined about his time slots. When he saw that Moushumi's early departure was detrimental to the progress of *Koshish*, he approached Sippy and began to discuss the possibility of a replacement. Sippy suggested that he cast Jaya Bhaduri for the role. Having worked with her in her debut film *Guddi* (1971), he knew she was a capable actress. As Raj Sippy recalls fondly, his father called Jaya Bhaduri and offered her the role. Such was her trust in him that she agreed without asking for clarifications about the subject of the film or even her fees. Due to technical problems, the set had to be shifted from Mohan Studio to Nataraj Studio and shooting resumed with Sanjeev Kumar opposite Jaya Bhaduri. The two got along very well as co-actors, simultaneously playing father and daughter in *Parichay* (1972) and a married couple in *Koshish*. A few years later, Sanjeev Kumar played Jaya Bhaduri's father-in-law in *Sholay* (1975). In *Naya Din Nayee Raat* (1974), Jaya was the only actress cast opposite Sanjeev Kumar, who played nine roles. She still remembers with admiration that while it was occasionally difficult for her to transition from one role to the other, Sanjeev was never discomfited by the changing nature of their relationships on screen.

But years later, the tables turned when Jaya was replaced by Moushumi in Gulzar's *Angoor*. The film industry is a very unpredictable place.

To Gulzar's initial disappointment, Sanjeev Kumar himself would often arrive late to the sets. Nevertheless, it was to his credit that he required minimal preparation and nearly always delivered perfectly on the first take itself. Gulzar still remembers his anger at finding Sanjeev late, claiming that he 'felt like hitting him', but the charming actor's smile always calmed him down. After one take, the director would always be reminded of what a wonderful actor they had the chance to work with. According to the film-maker himself:

> If other actors took an entire shift to complete their work for the day, Hari would complete the same in half the time.

Whenever Gulzar explained the scene to Sanjeev before it was shot, the actor seemed distracted, only half listening to his instructions. But when he performed, he left everyone stunned by the power of his delivery. This seemed to be a working pattern for Sanjeev Kumar. During the making of *Anhonee* (1973), Ravi Tandon was assailed by the same doubts, since Sanjeev never asked the assistant director to repeat his dialogues. It was only when the crew saw him perform with ease in front of the camera that they realized the true measure of his talent. Of the many directors he worked with, it was probably Hrishikesh Mukherjee who had the most faith in Sanjeev's ability to grasp what a role required. He never explained a scene in great detail to him; once he had explained the situation, he gave the actor carte blanche to perform as he pleased.

Koshish was completed within the stipulated time frame and when the film was released, it was appreciated by one and all. It became the second film for which Sanjeev Kumar would receive the prestigious National Award. The actor Raaj Kumar, who had never worked with Sanjeev and was known to be reticent about his fellow actors' talents, with the notable exception of Dilip Kumar, was effusive in his praise of Sanjeev's performance in the film. Years later, when his secretary S.P. Mahendra was producing *Angaaray* (1977), Raaj Kumar suggested that he cast Sanjeev Kumar in the film. The actress Jayaprada recalls working with the director K. Viswanath for the Telugu drama *Siri Siri Muvva* (1976) a few years later, in which she played a mute woman. The film was later remade in Hindi as

Sargam (1979). Apprehensive of the challenges the role faced, she fell back on her memories of having watched Sanjeev and Jaya Bhaduri in *Koshish*.

Sarika too, one of Sanjeev's harshest critics, could find no faults in *Koshish*. His performance in the movie proved his capabilities once and for all, since he could evoke so many emotions without leaning on any dialogues. With merely his actions and expressions, he brought a particular quality to the role that perhaps no other actor could have. *Koshish* was one of the crowning achievements of Sanjeev's illustrious career, so much so that, following his death, the Filmotsav held in Hyderabad in 1986 began with the screening of the film.

Sanjeev Kumar was always keen to play challenging roles. He was very eager to play Mirza Ghalib when Gulzar was contemplating a movie on the famous poet. It seems not only Sanjeev Kumar but also a certain college student was very interested in playing the title role in Gulzar's *Mirza Ghalib*. He took the liberty of writing a letter to Gulzar and explaining why Sanjeev Kumar, who according to him had no knowledge of Urdu and lacked a sense of poetry, was a very poor choice for Ghalib. Instead of Sanjeev Kumar, the young man urged Gulzar to cast him as Ghalib because only he understood the poet thoroughly. Gulzar didn't pay much heed to the letter then, but it stayed in his mind. The movie on Ghalib couldn't be made due to various reasons, but Gulzar did make a TV series on Ghalib after Sanjeev Kumar's death. The actor Gulzar chose to play Ghalib was Naseeruddin Shah, and Gulzar would later learn that it was Shah who had sent that letter asking Gulzar to choose him as his Ghalib many years ago.

Sholay (1975): The Film of the Millennium

Sholay, the film that changed the landscape of Indian cinema for years to come, was the product of a four-line idea the writer duo Salim–Javed approached the Sippys with. G.P. Sippy was a successful producer by then, but he noticed the potential of the story and decided to take a gamble on it. Looking to make a multistarrer, he told Salim–Javed to develop their idea.

Once the bare bones of the plot had been filled out, Sanjeev Kumar was the obvious choice to play the pivotal role of Thakur. Following the success of *Seeta Aur Geeta* (1972), Hema Malini and Dharmendra's sizzling chemistry was sure to be included as well. The problem was the second male lead. While Amitabh Bachchan was a strong contender for the part, he was far from the star he was to become. When shooting commenced in 1973, he was still considered an unbankable actor with a string of flops. Distributors were clamouring for Shatrughan Sinha to take the role, but Ramesh Sippy insisted on Bachchan playing Jay. Incidentally, Gabbar Singh was to be played by Danny Denzongpa, but he could not take up the role due to a prior commitment to Feroz Khan's *Dharmatma* (1975). For the iconic dance song 'Mehbooba Mehbooba', Jayshree T. was being considered, but Helen got the part, perhaps on Salim Khan's insistence. Everyone who had been cast knew that they were part of something huge, but none could have anticipated the phenomenal success the film would achieve.

The setting of the film itself set it apart from the dacoit films of the era. While film-makers usually flocked to Rajasthan in an effort to evoke the Chambal Valley landscape, Ramesh Sippy and art director Ram Yedekar settled on the hilly expanses of Ramanagaram, one hour away from the city of Bangalore. This maverick choice brought its own set of problems with it—an entire village had to be constructed from scratch. Roads, huts, telephone lines were to be built within two months and on a limited budget. The set's construction manager, Aziz Hanif Sheikh, meticulously planned the set, so that Gabbar's lair was directly behind Thakur's house, and the crew could easily cover the distance on foot. The villagers' huts doubled as make-up rooms with attached toilets and drainage. With a cast and crew numbering nearly a thousand, a godown and kitchen were also built to cater to their needs. The horses for the shoot were sourced from the police department or the Mysore Race Course and housed in a barn built by Sheikh. However, a few sequences were shot in more traditional locales. For example, the jail set was made at Rajkamal Kalamandir Studio in Bombay, while 'Mehbooba Mehbooba' was shot at RK Studio in Chembur.

As soon as the sets had been built and Danny had backed out of the project, Sanjeev Kumar suggested the newbie Amjad Khan to a worried Ramesh Sippy for the role. Javed Akhtar had some misgivings, convinced that a newcomer among five seasoned artistes might tilt the balance of the film, but the film went ahead with Amjad Khan. Sanjeev Kumar was responsible for the casting of another small character in the film—Arvind Joshi, who played his son. Amjad Khan came on board with his own inputs—it was his suggestion that the character of Gabbar Singh wear a costume akin to army fatigues, instead of the dhoti–kurta–tilak combination that was customary for dacoit films of the era.

Although 2 October 1973 had been fixed as the date for the shooting to begin, heavy rains disrupted the process. The first shot was taken on the next day, with the newly-weds Amitabh and Jaya Bachchan, who happened to be expecting their first child at the time. Sanjeev Kumar's first shot was with Amitabh and Dharmendra, a powerful exchange where Thakur cautions Jay and Veeru to bring Gabbar to him alive. Worried about his film, one of the costliest movies of the time, Sippy requested all the artistes to give him bulk dates, even allowing them to shoot for other films, provided they remained in Bangalore. The director Gulzar was worried about Sanjeev's involvement in *Sholay*, since he was simultaneously working with him in his film *Aandhi* (1975).

He asked him what his role was and why he was willing to star in a film in which he had no songs, no romantic scenes, and had to share the limelight with numerous other stars. Sanjeev Kumar explained to him that he had been drawn to the role because of the powerful scenes it would allow him to command. Later, Gulzar admitted, *Sholay* turned out to be Sanjeev and Amjad's film.

Due to Sanjeev Kumar and Hema Malini's personal differences, Dharmendra, Hema Malini, Amitabh Bachchan, Jaya Bhaduri, cinematographer Dwarka Diwecha and Ramesh Sippy stayed in a separate hotel, while Sanjeev Kumar put up with Arvind Joshi, Geeta Siddharth, Mac Mohan, A.K. Hangal, Sachin and Amjad Khan in another. All of them were friends from theatre, and Mac Mohan remembered them sitting down for a drink each evening after the shoot.

As Mac Mohan recalled in Anupama Chopra's *Sholay: The Making of a Classic*:

> Hari bhai was the quintessential night bird. Inordinately fond of drink, he would start late and continue long after the others had called it a night. His dinner would have to be repeatedly reheated. But Hari bhai never grew mean with alcohol. On the contrary, his smile grew wider and wider, until he would stop talking altogether and just smile.

The shooting for the film was finally completed by 22 April 1975. Helen and Jalal Agha were the last to face the camera. A long post-production period followed, since the film was made in 70 mm with six-track stereophonic sound effects. The director Ramesh Sippy was set on using 70 mm to capture the expanse of the landscape, and the thrill of the horses running across it.

Due to the violence depicted on screen, *Sholay* was held up by the censor board. Ramesh Sippy defended his film, saying that the film did not depict actual violence but suggested it symbolically, but the board remained adamant, and a few cuts had to be made. The climax of the film, meant to suggest the futility of revenge, was eventually scrapped. Sanjeev Kumar had to return from a trip to a film festival to reshoot the final sequence.

Sholay was released on 15 August 1975 and almost immediately declared a flop by film pundits. Rumours were rife that the Sippys were preparing to leave the country. The actor Jankidas remarked that Ramesh Sippy had unleashed five lions—Amitabh Bachchan, Sanjeev Kumar, Dharmendra, Hema Malini and Jaya Bhaduri—on a mouse, presumably Amjad Khan. G.P. Sippy called an emergency meeting to discuss what could be done to salvage the film. Javed Akhtar suggested dubbing Amjad Khan's dialogues with Kader Khan's voice. The actor did not agree, leading to an argument. Sanjeev Kumar supported Akhtar, causing a rift in his relationship with Amjad Khan.

In a surprising turn of events, *Sholay*'s earnings began to spike from the third week of its release. Soon, the film was hailed as a trailblazer and an instant classic by many. According to Vinay Sinha, Amjad Khan's secretary, Javed Akhtar changed his mind as well once the film was a hit, and even claimed in public that they had helped make the new actor's career. Amjad Khan and Salim–Javed did not work together again. As the film's collections shot up steadily, Khan asked his brother,

Who is the mouse now? Me, or the one who criticized my work?

The film's dialogues were so popular that fans can still recite them from memory, nearly five decades after the release. It holds the distinction of being the first film for which Polydor marketed a record of its dialogues. Remarkably, these records sold out fast and were played at gatherings ranging from festivals to weddings. Queues outside the theatres would stretch for kilometres, and 240 weeks into its release, theatres ran houseful. Making Rs 35 crore at the box office in its first run, *Sholay* made its way into the annals of Indian film history. Its massive earning was only rivalled two decades later with the release of Barjatya's *Hum Aapke Hain Koun..!* (1994). In *Sholay: The Making of a Classic*, Anupama Chopra notes that:

Sholay has been used to sell everything, from glucose biscuits to gripe water. Copywriters are still milking it dry.

Sholay's distributor, Suresh Kumar, aptly compared the film to the Taj Mahal, stating that every few years a new generation discovers its pleasures afresh.

Trishul (1978)

The reception of ground-breaking films, like *Anand* (1971), *Parichay* (1972), *Koshish* (1972), *Zanjeer* (1973), *Sholay* (1975) and *Aandhi* (1975), assured film-makers of a newfound maturity among their audiences. No longer were films afraid to challenge authority and address uncomfortable questions to the prevailing structures of society. By the mid-1970s, heart-warming romances were on their way out, with revenge actioners taking their place. Salim–Javed had found their niche, and with their unerring ability to capture the zeitgeist, they came up with another remarkable script.

The producer Gulshan Rai, meanwhile, still riding the waves of success post *Deewar* (1975), was eager to work with Yash Chopra again. When Salim–Javed presented the two with the script for *Trishul*, they accepted it enthusiastically.

Already typecast as the angry young man, Bachchan was the first choice to play the lead. However, initially, it proved difficult to find actors who could play his parents. Salim Khan asked Javed Akhtar to convince Vyjayanthimala to play Bachchan's mother, but the veteran actress had already refused to play the same role in *Deewaar*. Gulshan Rai and Yash Chopra, on the other hand, were torn between Nirupa Roy and Waheeda Rehman for the role. Casting Vijay's father posed an even greater challenge—his importance to the plot necessitated an actor who could carry the weight of being nearly the second lead to Bachchan's Vijay. Although Kulbhushan Kharbanda, Pran and Prem Nath were considered for the role, it fell to Sanjeev Kumar in the end. However, when the team approached Sanjeev Kumar, he demanded a fee higher than Bachchan's. To his understanding, he was a senior artiste, and no one could play the role with his gravitas. The team was at a loss; Amitabh Bachchan's market price numbered anywhere between Rs 6–8 lakh, and the budget for the film had been fixed at Rs 70 lakh. As Ramesh Talwar remembers, the matter was finally resolved when Sanjeev Kumar agreed to work for the same amount as Bachchan. Thus, *Trishul* became the first film for which the producer paid the rising star Amitabh Bachchan and Sanjeev Kumar the same amount.

Soon, a special office set was made at the Rajkamal Kalamandir Studio in Parel. When the shooting began, Sanjeev Kumar ran into his old friend Ramesh Talwar, then the assistant director to Yash Chopra. Talwar fondly remembered the star's humility and his famous ability to recall dialogues.

The sets of *Trishul*, like those of other films, were the setting for numerous memorable incidents. On one occasion, caught without his trousers ironed for a scene with Shashi Kapoor that had to be rushed—Kapoor wanted to leave the sets early—Sanjeev Kumar emerged from his make-up room dressed in a lungi under his shirt and tie. He asked the director to take a half shot, but Shashi Kapoor was in splits and could barely articulate his dialogues. After two retakes, Sanjeev Kumar turned to Shashi and told him that if he was late he would have no one to blame but himself.

Dedicated to the verisimilitude of the character he was creating on screen, Sanjeev Kumar would spend five or six hours in the make-up room trying to get his 'look' right. His make-up man Sarosh Modi played a stellar role and worked with Sanjeev Kumar in several of his movies: *Raja Aur Runk* (1968), *Khilona, Aandhi, Jaani Dushman* (1979), *Mausam* (1975), and many others.

Gulshan Rai had ordered seven to eight suits as costumes for the actors. This included a three-piece suit for Sanjeev Kumar, designed and made by Kachins, the tailor of Amitabh Bachchan's choice. Kumar was so impressed by his costume that, as Talwar recalled, he asked the producer if he could keep the suits. Although the actor offered to pay for them from his own remuneration, Rai presented them all to him as a gift.

Despite these isolated instances, Sanjeev Kumar was never a vain man. He often arrived at parties in his kurta and lungi. When his friends asked him why he did not dress well, he would tell them it did not matter to him. He had a few indulgences, however, and collecting lighters was one of them, according to his friend, actor Mahesh Desai. His humility and quiet confidence were further demonstrated by his willingness to compliment his co-stars on their work and even offer constructive feedback. He would chip in with inputs for the entire project, and praised the actor Prem Chopra for one of his shots profusely.

Although *Trishul* was a multistarrer made by a reputable director and backed by a big production house, Sanjeev had a premonition that the film wouldn't do well at the box office. His nephew Uday Jariwala remembers his uncle being unsure of the success of the film, saying that he liked his role but could not bring himself to be entirely confident of it. After the premiere, Dilip Kumar praised him, telling him that he was 'proud' of his work, a compliment Sanjeev Kumar treasured for the rest of his life.

When *Trishul* released, it was declared a superhit at the box office and critics and the audience alike appreciated Sanjeev Kumar and Amitabh Bachchan's emotionally charged performances. Following its success, *Trishul* was remade in Tamil and Malayalam and was nominated in five categories at the Filmfare Awards: Best Film, Best Director, Best Actor, Best Story and Best Supporting Actor.

Pati Patni Aur Woh (1978)

Sanjeev Kumar had always aspired to work with B.R. Chopra, especially after he missed an opportunity to do so in *Aadmi Aur Insaan* (1969). However, Chopra, by the late 1970s, was reeling from several losses. Although the modestly made *Chhoti Si Baat* (1975) had proved to be a hit, his son Ravi Chopra's debut film *Zameer* (1975) and *Karm* (1977) were both flops, despite the presence of stars like Amitabh Bachchan and Rajesh Khanna. A prescient man, Chopra soon grasped that films like *Sajjo Rani* (1976), *Chitchor* (1976) and *Gharonda* (1977) were finding the success that films with larger budgets missed. He decided to embark on a fresh project with a smaller budget to recover his losses from *Zameer* and *Karm*.

The writer Kamleshwar narrated a tale of marital infidelity to the producer. Although the story seemed fresh, it contained the elements of an action blockbuster, which Chopra was desperate to avoid. Looking for a light-hearted, feel-good comedy, he asked Kamleshwar to rewrite the story only retaining the central plot of infidelity.

With this new script, B.R. Chopra hoped to repeat the formula that had worked with *Chhoti Si Baat*. Basu Chatterjee was to direct the lead pair of Sanjeev Kumar and Vidya Sinha. Unfortunately, Chatterjee was busy directing *Tumhare Liye* (1978), starring Vidya Sinha and Sanjeev Kumar. Ravi Chopra was caught up with *Tumhari Kassam* (1978), and thus B.R. Chopra decided to take up the reins of director himself. Sanjeev Kumar and Vidya Sinha's chemistry was already apparent in two of Raj Tilak's films, so he decided to cast them. For the second lead, however, he wanted a fresh face, and Ranjeeta Kaur fit the bill perfectly for the role of the pretty, young secretary.

When Chopra approached Sanjeev Kumar with the film, the actor agreed immediately. He had been looking forward to working with the producer for a long time, and even turned down a proposal from the south for a film which purportedly would have paid him a great deal more.

Although most of Chopra's first choices for actors and crew members had not worked out, the film was ready to hit the floor with Asrani in place to play Sanjeev's sidekick and Ravindra Jain roped in for the music. The first shot for the film was taken, with Sanjeev Kumar, Vidya Sinha and Master Bittu, in a Juhu bungalow. A prankster by heart, Sanjeev Kumar insisted on the shot being retaken a number of times since it included a near-kiss with the leading lady!

Vidya Sinha says:

During the making of *Pati Patni Aur Woh*, we didn't realize that we were working for a film. It was a picnic atmosphere on the sets.

And Ranjeeta Kaur asserted:

> I enjoyed working in *Pati Patni Aur Woh* as well, especially with
> Sanjeev Sahib.

Both off and on screen, Sanjeev Kumar was a humorous man, never
unwilling to laugh at himself or at others, and Ramesh Talwar
remembered him joking around about Yunus Parvez and Mac
Mohan. During shoots, he would embrace the occasional sequence
that would make him appear funny or even ridiculous. Although years
of heavy drinking and unhealthy food habits had taken their toll on
his body, he performed with ease for the song 'Thande Thande Paani
Se', which required him to appear clad only in his *chaddi* or shorts.
His complete lack of self-consciousness ensured the song's timeless
appeal. The dancer–actress Jayshree T. also remembers Sanjeev
Kumar as a humble, humorous man. When they were in Amritsar
doing a stage show together, the stage collapsed, and Sanjeev fell
with it. Everyone watched with bated breath, terrified that the star
would lose his temper. To their surprise, he came out of the wreckage
laughing, making light of the whole matter.

Sanjeev Kumar made everyone around him feel immediately at
ease. Sarika's 'Hari Uncle' seemed an easy-going man, who never
expressed his inner turmoil to anyone.

Upon being asked what makes a good actor, Sanjeev Kumar
had once responded: a good voice, and a capability for complete
insolence. His performance in *Pati Patni Aur Woh* demonstrated that
he was gifted with both. The writer Javed Siddiqui thought of him as
a 'king of comedy', who shone in films like *Pati Patni Aur Woh* and
Angoor (1981).

Once, when asked:

> What are the qualifications required to become a good actor?

he laughed and replied:

People say good looks, smartness, etc., can help one become a good actor, but these aren't necessary. As far as acting is concerned, everyone is a good actor, the talent is brought out by suffering. Students act in front of the teachers and criminals act in front of the cops to avoid punishment; many mothers-in-law and daughters-in-law act to gain sympathy and importance in the family. We are all constantly acting, according to our requirements.

His attitude translated easily on to the screen as well. Once again, he managed to win the audience over as a faithless husband in *Pati Patni Aur Woh*. The film proved to be a superhit at the box office and ran at Dreamland Cinema in Mumbai for over thirty weeks. Kamleshwar won the Filmfare Award for Best Screenplay, while the leading pair was nominated for the Best Actor and Best Actress awards.

Shatranj Ke Khilari (1977)

Renowned film-maker Satyajit Ray was so taken with *Sholay* on his first viewing that he returned for another show the very same day. As the film worked its magic, the auteur's eyes were fixed on two actors in particular—Sanjeev Kumar and Amjad Khan.

It was producer Suresh Jindal who suggested Amjad Khan for the role of Nawab Wajid Ali Shah to Satyajit Ray. Following *Sholay*, he was a major box-office draw, and Jindal found that he bore an uncanny resemblance to the personage himself. Amjad Khan, who would go on to be known for his villainous roles, outdid himself as the gentle Wajid Ali Shah.

As soon as Ray reached Kolkata, he sat down to make sketches of Amjad Khan in Wajid Ali Shah's costumes. While researching for a film, Ray left no stone unturned. His workspace overflowed with books on the era, and the director would sketch out the characters as they took shape around his research. His sketches of Amjad Khan in costume turned out to be a dead ringer for the nawab. According to Suresh Jindal:

Ray was a tireless and outstanding researcher. His mind was like a steel trap, focused only on the subject at hand. Every available space in his study was now piled high with books on chess, James Outram's Blue Books, books of Company School paintings, other master printmakers and painters of Indian landscapes and architecture, miscellaneous travelogues and every other kind of information on the period in which the story was set.

Working on the film for Jindal was like a 'magical mystery tour', involving trips to museums, havelis in Lucknow, thakur baris in north Calcutta, dinner with the dowager queen of Jaipur and searches for experts on the Shia namaz in the winding alleys of old Lucknow.

Ray chose Sanjeev Kumar and Saeed Jaffrey to play the two noblemen Mirza Sajjad Ali and Mir Roshan Ali. Shabana Azmi played Mirza's much-neglected wife, Khurshid, while Farida Jalal was Nafisa, Mir's wife who finds solace in an extramarital affair. The veteran actor Sir Richard Attenborough brought General Outram to the screen. Although Ray was hesitant to offer such a small role to the reputed actor, he believed him to be the only man who could do it justice. As Jindal writes, Attenborough is said to have exclaimed:

Satyajit, I would be happy to recite even the telephone directory for you!

Satyajit Ray had an uncanny ability to judge actors. In an interview with me, he said he only noticed two things in an actor: the eyes and the walk.

Javed Siddiqui was appointed to write the dialogues for the film, keeping in mind his expertise in Urdu. He was also assigned to improve Sanjeev Kumar's pronunciation of the language. This was the first time the writer was working with Sanjeev Kumar, and he was amazed at the keen attention the actor paid to each shot and scene. Often, he would approach Siddiqui to practise the delivery of particular dialogues. Although he was already a star, and his market price had skyrocketed to several lakhs, he remained a humble, hard-working actor all his life.

Notoriously late to the sets for most other films, Sanjeev Kumar was immensely punctual while working with Ray, excited to be part of such a project. Jindal had assigned a separate car to convey him to the sets, and Sanjeev would be up and ready to go even before the car could arrive at the hotel. According to most sources, he worked on *Shatranj Ke Khilari* for very little remuneration, since he believed working with Satyajit Ray to be a once-in-a-lifetime opportunity.

During the making of the film, Shabana Azmi was asked how much she was being paid to star in the film. She responded that money meant nothing to her, and that she would even chop off her right hand to do a Ray film. Ever the prankster, Sanjeev replied:

Well, I can't cut my hand off, it has already been lopped off by Ramesh Sippy for *Sholay*.

Once the laughter had subsided, he said on a more serious note:

Any actor who puts money before Ray's film would be a fool.

Suresh Jindal also recalls:

When I told Shabana Azmi, a gifted actress with several memorable films to her credit, that her role in *Shatranj Ke Khilari* would be limited to two or three scenes, she replied: 'Suresh, if Ray wants me to hold a *jhadu* for one shot only, I will gladly do it. Work with Ray? Wow!'

The first shot taken for the film was of Sanjeev Kumar and Saeed Jaffrey playing chess. Although the script did not mention any extraneous gestures, Sanjeev Kumar improvised while shooting. As soon as the camera started rolling, he looked completely absorbed in the game. Lost in thought, he stroked his eyebrows, and plucked a single hair and rolled it between his fingers for a while before making his next move. The gesture was so natural that even Ray was impressed with Sanjeev's ingenious addition. According to Farida Jalal, who played Nafisa in the film:

> This could only be done by an actor who is committed to his work and is concerned about the betterment of the project.

Unfortunately, creative differences soon erupted between Saeed Jaffrey and Sanjeev Kumar. While Sanjeev Kumar preferred to rehearse a shot multiple times before he faced the camera, Jaffrey felt that too many rehearsals would rob his performance of spontaneity. Shoots were cancelled for a day, and a tense Ray called for a meeting to resolve the problem. Attenborough came up with a solution: Saeed would sit by himself in a corner while Sanjeev rehearsed with Siddiqui. As soon as Sanjeev felt sufficiently ready, they would join each other for a technical rehearsal before the take.

Sanjeev had his own method, and this had hardly changed since his days at the IPTA. During the first rehearsal he only learnt his dialogues and tried out the gestures, on the second rehearsal he delivered his dialogues from memory and did not concentrate on any expression, on the third rehearsal he delivered dialogues with the right expression and continued with it until he was absolutely satisfied with himself; he had to feel like he had internalized the character so well that his entity and the character's had fused into one. And only then would he ask for the final take.

Dedicated to his craft as he was, Sanjeev Kumar had only one weakness—good food. According to Sarika, actresses who were fond of Sanjeev Kumar would often cook his favourites and send them to his shoots, aware that he wanted to marry a woman who could cook good food. While in Calcutta for the shooting of the film, he would ask Siddiqui for recommendations and take his friends out for dinner. On one such occasion, he decided to go to a renowned dhaba in the city. When he arrived at the eatery, along with Siddiqui and his other friends, he was amazed to discover that the establishment was run by a family. He was so impressed that he asked the entire family to join him at his table, making for an unforgettable meal.

While *Shatranj Ke Khilari* was still in the making, news arrived of Amjad Khan's accident. His car had crashed into a tree on the Mumbai–Goa road on 15 October 1976, the day of his brother Imtiaz Khan's birthday. The accident left him with broken ribs and a punctured lung. Despite the schedules for the film being affected, Ray remained set on Amjad Khan as the nawab and waited for him to recover. Fortunately, Amjad recovered quickly and was soon back in Calcutta shooting for *Shatranj Ke Khilari* again.

Away from his family for so long, Sanjeev Kumar began to grow restless in Kolkata. As soon as the film was near completion, he asked Siddiqui if he could wrap up his shots quickly, since he was expected to return to Bombay and shoot for Vishwamitter Adil's *Inspector Eagle* (1978). A week later, Siddiqui mentioned this to Adil, only to find out that Sanjeev often used his name as an excuse to leave when he grew weary of a place.

Silsila (1981)

Sagar Sarhadi is said to have once narrated a story of two young couples to Pamela Chopra. The story moved her so much that she shared it with her husband, Yash. A seasoned producer, Chopra saw the story for what it was and asked Sarhadi to develop it further, thus providing the impetus for the writing of *Silsila*.

Chopra decided to direct the film, casting his favourite actors Amitabh Bachchan and Shashi Kapoor as the male leads. He also signed on Smita Patil. Parveen Babi, who had already worked with Chopra for *Deewaar* (1975) and *Kaala Patthar* (1979), was chosen on Bachchan's recommendation. Parveen Babi and Amitabh Bachchan soon left for Kashmir to shoot for *Kaalia* (1981), preceding the rest of the crew. The actress was so enthusiastic about being a part of *Silsila* that she took the costumes for the upcoming film with her.

Unfortunately, during the filming of *Kaalia*, Amitabh noticed that his co-star did not seem well. Her voice sounded different, and she looked like she had not slept at all. Assuming that heavy drinking was affecting her, he called Yash Chopra to Kashmir to decide what was to be done. Chopra was deeply disturbed to see the state Parveen Babi was in. Would this affect the future of his multistarrer? With no other way out, he visited her hotel room and informed her that the script for *Silsila* had undergone many changes, and she could no longer star in the film. According to Sagar Sarhadi and later confirmed by Pravin Bhatt, an enraged Parveen Babi blamed Bachchan for the incident, accusing him of kidnapping her and even planting a chip in her face.

Parveen Babi's erratic behaviour was to become the talk of the town. I once had the opportunity to be present during an interview with her. Having just been introduced to each other, Parveen then proceeded to size the interviewer up and declare:

I know him since a long time.

Later, the same day, upon glancing at a magazine cover with a picture of Raj Babbar on it, Parveen asked:

Who is he?

evidently unable to recognize the renowned actor and her co-star in *Arpan* (1983), even when prompted.

Bizarrely, the next day, Parveen asked the interviewer to come to her flat. The interviewer did as instructed and returned carrying roughly 200 copies of an unknown document drafted by Parveen. Upon investigation, these turned out to be unbelievable accusations against Amitabh Bachchan. Sadly, Parveen Babi was soon diagnosed with schizophrenia, an acute mental disorder.

Meanwhile, Sanjeev Kumar had already been cast to play Chandni's husband in the film. Following Parveen Babi's dismissal, however, the film was missing a Chandni. While Chopra wanted to cast Rekha in the role, he was doubtful of having her play the 'other woman' opposite Amitabh Bachchan. Sanjeev suggested a solution: if Jaya Bachchan were to play the role of Bachchan's onscreen wife Shobha, who remains steadfastly by her husband's side despite his infidelity, the film would gain some traction considering the rumours that were already circulating in the tabloids about the Bachchan couple.

Yash Chopra was immensely pleased with the idea, anticipating the publicity the film would receive even before it hit the theatres. Sanjeev set about convincing his friend and erstwhile co-actor Jaya Bachchan to appear in the film. Meeting her at her bungalow, he explained to her the opportunities the film would offer and assured her that there would be complete professionalism on the sets. Tentatively, he also suggested that working so closely with her husband might help resolve their marital problems. Jaya agreed to appear as Shobha on the condition that she be allowed to remain on the set even when she was not required. As soon as the cast had been finalized, Shashi Kapoor informed Smita Patil of the decision, and she stepped out of the film gracefully. With some adjustments on the parts of all the stars, the dates for the shoots were soon lined up.

Despite the powerhouse casting of Amitabh–Rekha–Jaya, Sanjeev Kumar made his presence felt and walked away with the accolades. Although Amitabh Bachchan's rendition made 'Rang Barse' the song it is, people watching it even today agree that Sanjeev Kumar's performance added layers to it and to the narrative. However, the film did not do very well at the box office. Chopra's hopeful predictions for the production only bore fruit years later, as the film gradually gained a cult following.

Angoor (1982)

Gulzar's *Angoor* enjoyed a long cinematic and literary history preceding it, decades before it came to the screen in 1981. Shakespeare's *The Comedy of Errors* inspired Ishwar Chandra Vidyasagar's play

Bhrantibilas. In 1963, the play was adapted into the Uttam Kumar–Sabitri Chatterjee starrer of the same name. Soon after, Bimal Roy produced *Do Dooni Chaar* (1968) in Hindi, based on the Bengali film, only to see it fail at the box office.

Gulzar himself had had a long association with the story. Smitten by the bard's play, he had already penned a script based on it, which served as the screenplay for Bimal Roy's venture. The film's dismal failure left a mark on the writer: it seemed to be a project he could not do justice to. Not one to give up, he returned to the script and rewrote it, tidying the plot, tying up any loose ends he had left the first time round. *Angoor*'s moment to shine came soon after Gulzar's *Kitaab* (1977), which did not do very well at the box office. Producer Jai Singh, presciently observing the profitable union of a classic tale from Shakespeare and Gulzar's seasoned craftsmanship, took a gamble on the script. With the movie in the works, Sanjeev Kumar and Moushumi Chatterjee were cast in the lead roles. Upon Sanjeev's suggestion, Deven Verma was cast in the role of Bahadur.

A large chunk of *Angoor*'s success can be attributed to its ingenious star cast. Sanjeev Kumar's gift in slipping in and out of characters effortlessly, Deven Verma's flawless sense of timing, Moushumi Chatterjee's priceless expressions, coupled with Gulzar's sharp sense of wit and catchy one-liners all blended to turn *Angoor* into an utterly delectable comedy. *Angoor* tells the story of two pairs of twins who get separated in childhood only to reunite as grown-ups. Brimming over with hilarious mix-ups between husband and wife, master and attendant, and sprinkled generously with clever dialogues delivered with maximum comical impact, Gulzar's fine artistry is reflected in every frame of *Angoor*. In the end, however, it is his meticulous attention to detail that shines through. Every character is neatly etched, with the actors having received definitive clues to differentiate between the sets of twins.

Gulzar had the uncanny gift of looking beyond stereotypes. His *Parichay, Khushboo* and *Kinara* helped Jeetendra break out of his dancing-in-white-trousers avatar. Even though Sanjeev Kumar had never been typecast, no other director was as successful as Gulzar in allowing him to try out such a large spectrum of characters.

Gulzar's *Angoor* captivated its audience and left them in splits, becoming a superhit at the box office on its release. According to the actress Sharmila Tagore, the film's impeccable comic timing, and the precision of both Sanjeev Kumar and Deven Verma's performances, made the film immensely popular. *Angoor* earned the actor Deven Verma the Best Comic Actor award and Sanjeev Kumar a nomination for the Best Actor award at the thirtieth Filmfare Awards.

Namkeen (1982): Sanjeev's Last Film with Gulzar

Gulzar, the perfectionist, made it a habit of sticking with a project until he felt he had done complete justice to it, sometimes revisiting it even after completion. The fire raged on within him until it attained his own stamp of approval. It had happened before for *Do Dooni Char* (1968), and it would happen again for *Kitaab* (1977).

After *Kitaab* let Gulzar down at the box office, he returned to Samaresh Basu's oeuvre, this time choosing *Akal Basant*, a bittersweet narrative based on three young women and their strict disciplinarian mother, set in the rural outskirts of Himachal Pradesh, to craft *Namkeen*.

The casting of *Namkeen*, however, took a dramatic turn. Initially, Waheeda Rehman was to play the role of the matriarch while Rekha would essay the role of her eldest daughter. Rekha was producer Jayant Malkan's suggestion—a huge crowd-puller, she would be invaluable to the film. To those who doubted whether Waheeda Rehman would look convincing as Rekha's mother, Malkan said that if Amitabh Bachchan could play Rehman's son in *Trishul*, why couldn't Rekha play her daughter? Thus, Rekha came to be an integral part of the casting, while Shabana Azmi and Kiran Vairale were to play the other two sisters. Sanjeev Kumar, meanwhile, essayed the pivotal role of the truckdriver. As soon as all the actors were on board, Gulzar began his schedule for *Namkeen* at Mohan Studio, Andheri, where the set of a dilapidated house, detailed down to naked electric bulbs and abundant cobwebs, was constructed by art director Ajit Banerjee.

However, unbeknownst to Gulzar, his lead actress happened to be going through a personal crisis. Tabloid journalism was abuzz with salacious rumours concerning Rekha and Amitabh Bachchan, leading Bachchan to boycott all interaction with the media. Rekha was very upset as well, especially with freelance journalist H. Khaturiya, who had written extensively about the pair. One day, Khaturiya, a friend of Gulzar's, stepped into *Namkeen*'s set while Rekha was facing the camera with Waheeda Rehman, completely unannounced. Rekha stormed out of the set, with Gulzar in pursuit. A heated argument ensued when Rekha declared that she would not tolerate Khaturiya's presence and Gulzar in turn asserted that he wouldn't kick his friend off the sets. He tried to make her appreciate how the personal and the professional should be strictly compartmentalized. But Rekha wouldn't have any of it. Gulzar had to choose between his lead actress and his friend. He refused to budge from his stance, and Rekha, without informing her co-stars or notifying her director, left the studio for good. Producer Jayant Malkan and cinematographer M. Sampat tried to sort out the differences between Gulzar and Rekha, but to no avail.

Gulzar decided to cast Sharmila Tagore in Rekha's place. He had had a pleasant experience while working with her in *Mausam* (1975), a film for which she had also received a National Award. When Sharmila Tagore was informed about Gulzar's offer, sources say that she was so thrilled, she arrived at the sets the very next day without so much as asking for further details, and shooting resumed.

During one of my interviews with Kiran Vairale, published in the Marathi magazine *Mayur Pankh*, I asked her how she chanced upon Gulzar's *Namkeen*. She replied:

> Gulzar sahib was looking for a teenager to play the youngest daughter of Waheeda-ji. I think Shabana-ji advised him to watch my play, *Aakhri Sawal*, and that's how I got to work in *Namkeen*.

After Rekha's replacement, the situation at *Namkeen*'s sets was once again turbulent, due to Sanjeev Kumar's constant tardiness. Some days he arrived as much as six hours after the scheduled time, forcing all the actors, including veteran actress Waheeda Rehman, to wait for him. According to director Gulzar:

> I didn't like it. Not a single actor broke the discipline on my set except Sanjeev, and, on *Namkeen*'s set, I had problems with Waheeda-ji, Sharmila-ji and Shabana-ji, as they used to complain that I was being partial to him. One day, I told Sharmila-ji that as his seniors, why don't they talk to him? Why were they waiting for me? But I don't know what power he had over them, because as soon as he entered everyone went quiet and joined him without another word.

Sharmila Tagore adds,

> Waiting for him for hours, we'd lose our cool and speak against him, which was natural. During the making of *Mausam* we had faced the same problem. Once, would you believe, I had to wait for him for eight hours in full make-up? When he entered, I didn't speak to him and showed my anger by my expressions, but he did not react. He behaved as though nothing had happened, smiling his charming smile. He had a good quality, that he would never argue with anyone. Whoever had a problem with him would automatically calm down. We tolerated his late arrival because he was sweet and down-to-earth.

Surprisingly, Sanjeev Kumar, while an impeccably effortless actor, preferred using glycerine for emotional scenes. Sachin recounts:

> One day I asked him about this and he advised me to use glycerin as well, saying that natural tears don't shine on screen the way glycerin does.

Despite *Namkeen*'s daring plot, immaculate cast, authentic locations and attention to detail, it was an average hit. However, Essabhai M. Suratwala won the National Film Award for Best Audiography, Samaresh Basu won the Filmfare Award for Best Story, Ajit Banerjee won the Filmfare Award for Best Art Direction and both Waheeda Rehman and Kiran Vairale were nominated for Best Supporting Actress.

When the IPTA organized a premiere show for *Namkeen* at Dreamland Cinema, Bombay, on 1 April 1982, Sanjeev Kumar arrived with Gulzar and Kaifi Azmi to attend the screening. He smiled and waved and made his way inside the cinema with his dear friend Gulzar, little knowing that this would be their last venture together.

With an actor like Sanjeev Kumar, having a list of landmark films is a tough ask. More so when you consider the number of films he acted in and the variety of roles he essayed. We have spoken of *Naya Din Nayee Raat* elsewhere, and it remains a landmark performance in the annals of Indian cinema. Films like *Dastak* and *Anubhav* explored facets of the actor that the world of mainstream Hindi films rarely managed to. While *Manoranjan, Manchali* and *Biwi O Biwi* gave us an insight into his comic potential, his Filmfare Award-winning act in *Arjun Pandit* was another example of the range this actor of actors was capable of. If he held his own superbly against a superstar like Rajesh Khanna in *Aap Ki Kasam*, he did so with aplomb in *Hum Paanch*, in which he was ranged against a crop of young and upcoming stars. The list is endless, and the selection here is just a sampling of Sanjeev Kumar's finest.

16

Two Deaths That Changed Him

The sixth of November 1980, just another day at the Jariwala household. It was two in the afternoon and Kishore was watching a cricket match. Jyoti, after a busy morning of completing household chores, had found a moment of quiet and was taking a nap, while her husband Nikul was out. Gayatri had called, she was doing well in the US; Sanjeev had left Bombay for Hyderabad on the fourth and was probably engrossed in his shoot, memorizing and rehearsing his lines. The match had kept Kishore glued to the TV set, but he was afraid that if he delayed his bath any longer his mother would come in to give him an earful. He freshened up quickly, but where was his comb? He tiptoed into his mother's room, afraid to disturb her siesta, and there it was! He had just stepped towards the mirror, comb in hand, when his heart skipped a beat. He saw his mother's reflection, she was lying awkwardly, her dentures had fallen on the ground and there was something ominous about her perfect stillness. Something was not right. The comb fell from his nerveless fingers and he screamed for help.

Two days earlier, Sanjeev Kumar had been due to travel to film K. Bapaiah's *Takkar* (1980), in which he appeared alongside Jeetendra and Zeenat Aman. Before he left, he had touched his mother's feet, promising to call her every day. Shantaben had blessed him and said goodbye. Neither knew that it would be the last time they would see each other.

When Kishore raised the alarm, Jyoti came running to Shantaben's room. They immediately called Jamnadas over for help and rushed Shantaben to Nanavati Hospital. They reached the hospital at three in the afternoon, and by the evening, Jassu, Tarla Joshi and Dilip Dutt were there to support the family. Nikul was the last to see his mother alive. As he reached her side, she closed her eyes forever.

The family was at a loss; how would they convey this awful news to Sanjeev? Jamnadas informed Sanjeev that Shantaben was gravely ill, and that he must return at once. Sanjeev took the first flight home. When he finally saw her, Sanjeev Kumar broke down, shattered. He marked 6 November as a black day for the rest of his life, a date on which he would neither step out of the house nor shoot for a film. Shantaben's funeral was set for 7 November, and Sanjeev Kumar performed her last rites. According to actress Leena Chandavarkar, Sanjeev was inconsolable, looking like a lost child. Sanjeev was so devastated by his loss that he refused to touch food for nearly a whole week.

For Sanjeev Kumar, this pain was unbearable. His life had revolved almost entirely around his mother. He had seen her fight formidable circumstances and resuscitate the family business. His idol and champion both, she was invaluable to the actor. After her passing, he would secretly watch *Dumbo* (1941), the Disney animated feature film based on the story of a baby elephant that could fly. During the scene where the baby elephant gets separated from his mother, he would weep silently before the television, tearfully remembering his own mother and wishing he could have held her for one last time.

*

The evening of 18 September 1984 stood out as odd to Sanjeev Kumar's neighbour: the lights in his flat were on, and the door was open. Thinking of this as an opportunity to finally meet the star and offer him a cup of tea, he walked into the house. In the living room, to his dismay, lay Sanjeev's brother Nikul, completely motionless. He had just suffered a fatal cardiac arrest. He lay there with a pill in his hand, having been unable to take the medicine in time.

The day was also the Aatham day in the Gujarati calendar, the same day on which Sanjeev Kumar's father had passed away. Nikul's wife, Jyoti, had wanted to visit the Siddhi Vinayak temple to pray for her ailing husband. Earlier that year, Nikul had suffered his first cardiac arrest. The medical reports showed three blockages in his heart and the doctor advised a bypass surgery at the earliest. Sanjeev Kumar decided to take him to the United States for surgery within six months. Little did he know, his brother would not live to see that day. According to Jyoti Jariwala:

> In those days, very few people decided to operate abroad. Bhai took this decision because his sister was settled in the USA and because of the superior medical facilities in the US.

Meanwhile, Sanjeev would urge Nikul to take better care of himself, reminding him that he had a family to look after.

Sanjeev's and Nikul's passports were soon ready, and the trip was set to coincide with Sanjeev's planned tour to the US. In the meantime, the actor planned to meet Kailash Advani to discuss his upcoming project, titled *Ujala*.

On the morning of the eighteenth, Sanjeev left for a shoot at the Elephanta Caves. Prithvi, Nikul's seven-year-old son who wanted to accompany his uncle to the fascinating site, went with him. Later in the day, Jyoti and Nikul left Parin Villa together. Nikul was meant to air out Sanjeev's flat in Chadda House.

After he had tried, and had failed, to revive Nikul, Sanjeev's neighbour sent word to Parin Villa. Jyoti rushed to Chadda House on Khar Road with Jamnadas, while Kishore and his wife, Prafulla, hurried there with Tarla Joshi. But they were too late: by the time they arrived, Nikul had passed away, leaving behind his young widow and three children, Uday, Prithvi and Ekta.

Jamnadas informed Gayatri, but once again, everyone was at a loss as to how to convey the news to Sanjeev, who was still travelling with Prithvi. Ultimately, Jamnadas asked Johnny Whisky, an actor and close friend of Sanjeev, to bring Sanjeev back from the caves on the pretext that his brother had fallen gravely ill. Upon reaching Parin Villa, the presence of the small crowd at the gate alerted Sanjeev to what had transpired. The memory of his mother's passing still fresh in his mind, the actor suffered a mild heart attack as well.

As soon as he had collected himself, he dedicated his time to the care of Nikul's children. He also encouraged Jyoti to remarry, although she refused to do so. Her decision encouraged some tabloids to report a supposed relationship between the two, creating some tension in the household. A distant relative, Mumta Jariwala's mother-in-law Maltiben, came to stay with the two to set these rumours to rest.

Something went missing from Sanjeev Kumar's personality after the passing of his brother. It was like he had lost his zest for life. His charming smile, which had won the hearts of innumerable women, could hardly be seen on his face. He began to prefer seclusion over the company of friends and spent his time lost in his thoughts.

17

Off-Screen Hero

A lot has been written about Sanjeev Kumar—the ever-versatile actor who could fluidly step in and out of the most complex of characters—but not much is known about the kind of person he was. This chapter celebrates Sanjeev and looks at him sans the filmy make-up and harsh studio lights. This is about the flesh-and-blood person beyond the screen. Remember Naginbhai, the person who had tried to take everything from the Jariwalas after Sanjeev's father passed away? Years later, the same Naginbhai threw his brother Chaganbhai's family out of their house when Chaganbhai died, and it was Shantaben and Sanjeev who took Chaganbhai's daughter Prabha under their wing and enrolled her at KC College for further studies. Prabha Shah recalls:

> Because of Shantaben and Haribhai I could complete my education. He was so caring that he sent me and his own sister Gayatri by car to college, and he didn't allow us to wear shabby clothes.

Being the eldest son, he was aware of his responsibilities towards his brothers and sisters. Kishore completed his education from Sydenham College and Gayatri from Jai Hind College, respectively.

After he established himself in the industry post *Khilona*, Sanjeev Kumar organized the marriages of Gayatri and Nikul at his own expense. The lavish marriages took place on 10 and 11 December 1971 in Bombay.

Years later, when Kishore consented to getting married, Sanjeev immediately purchased a flat in his brother's name at Sangita Apartments, Juhu (as a part of his share in their late father Jethalal's property). Kishore and Prafulla's marriage was performed on 18 April 1982 in Bombay.

He was altogether a different person when it came to his family and very protective about their privacy. Even his friends did not know his family personally. Sarika recalls:

> I went to his place many times. But I never spoke to his sister-in-law or any other member. I only knew them by their faces.

While Nikul and Sanjeev's partnership was well recognized, his relationship with his brother Kishore is something not many talk about because Kishore refused to live under Sanjeev's shadow. Sanjeev had helped establish Nikul as a producer and film distributor, and he was willing to extend the same help to Kishore, but Kishore made it amply clear that he did not need Sanjeev's assistance. It had clearly become a matter of pride and Sanjeev knew better than to hurt his brother's ego, so he respectfully kept away. In fact, before marrying Prafulla, Kishore had warned:

> If you think you are marrying film star Sanjeev Kumar's brother, forget about this marriage.

It was difficult for Sanjeev to watch one brother prosper while the other struggled to make ends meet. Nikul was busy with film distributions while Kishore eked out a meagre living by acting in Gujarati plays and composing the occasional score for regional films. Hindi films were a long way away for Kishore, as was financial stability. Now it was mutually understood that Sanjeev would not come to Kishore's rescue because Kishore did not wish for his help. But Sanjeev, who had taken on the role of their absent father, could no longer pretend that this didn't bother him. So, Sanjeev set his sister, Gayatri, on a secret mission to find out what Kishore needed by casually visiting Kishore. Gayatri dutifully visited Kishore and Prafulla and noted down everything that the couple required and handed over the list to Sanjeev. Gayatri Patel recollects:

> As I reported to Bhai he gave me money and asked me to purchase all the necessary things and send them over to Kishore as gifts from my side; and he also instructed me to not mention his name at all. I did what Bhai asked me to do.

Sanjeev had invested in a lavish restaurant called Princess Hotel in Bangalore and he needed someone to look after the business. He could have easily asked Kishore, but knowing his obstinate nature, he offered the job to his brother-in-law, Ashok Patel. Sanjeev's real motive was to make his sister relocate to India so that they could all live close to one another. Remembering this time, Ashok Patel says:

> I was in India and I was supposed to stay here for some days to finalize the Hotel Princess project. But in between I got a call from my wife Gayatri and she informed me that she was diagnosed with breast cancer. It was a shocking news for me.

Sanjeev was devastated after hearing about his sister's condition and asked Ashok to be by her side. According to Gayatri Patel:

> I was lucky that my cancer was diagnosed early and without wasting any time we went ahead with the operation, which was successful. The doctor said that I would live for another ten years. But God is great, thirty-eight years have passed and I am still alive.

Whenever Gayatri came to visit from America, he sent Nikul to receive her at the airport. Gayatri Patel adds:

> And whenever I left for America, Bhai used to come with me at the airport and drop me inside the plane on my seat. He took special permission for this from the airport authority.

On the festival of Raksha Bandhan he made it a point to meet all of his sisters. Gayatri Patel passed away peacefully in her sleep on 17 February 2021 in the USA.

Gayatri would send him a rakhi all the way from the USA and the siblings would catch up over the phone. Many acquaintances came home to fasten their rakhis around his wrist, including Akhtar Bi (K. Asif's wife), Madhumati, Anju Mahendru, Mehmood's sister, Shano, and Minu Mumtaz. According to actress Madhumati:

> I became his rakhi sister during the making of our home production film, *Jai Jwala*. I approached him and offered a guest role. He was a busy star, but he agreed saying, 'I will do the guest role for my sister,' and the word sister appealed to me and I started tying him a rakhi on every Raksha Bandhan.

Anju Mahendru narrates a hilarious incident:

> Most of the time, my mother would be away in London for rakhi. So I'd end up tying a rakhi on Hari on her behalf. Once I told him, 'This time I won't take Rs 500. I want a gold tissue sari.' Those days the sari was a rage and cost Rs 2500. He said, 'Are you mad? There are ten sisters waiting outside!' I said I didn't care and that I wanted it. He said in his inimitable style, '*Paisa nahin hai*!'
>
> He then took his briefcase and threw it at me, asking me to check whether it had money. He thought I wouldn't open it. But I did and removed a bundle of notes and ran down from his house.

He called me from the second floor. He was smiling as he waved
the gold Dupont lighter that I had left behind (worth thousands)!

Sanjeev had a superstition. He always made sure that his family
never travelled together in the same car or plane. He, his mother and
nephew Uday went in one car, while his brother, Nikul, Nikul's wife,
Jyoti, and nephew Prithvi travelled in another car or flight.

He doted on his niece and nephews. Celebrating their birthdays
with much aplomb, letting them choose their gifts, taking them to
shoots, watching the latest Hollywood movies with them, Sanjeev
spent as much time with them as possible, even though he had a hectic
schedule. Sometimes he would wake up before they left for school or
stayed home to meet them in the evening if he had had an exceptionally
busy schedule that was keeping him away from the children. Ekta,
his two-and-a-half-year-old niece, whom he lovingly called '*dingli*'
(meaning doll), found a patient listener in her uncle who would pay
close attention to all her toddler woes concerning lost toys and petty
fights with great concern. According to sister-in-law Jyoti Jariwala:

> When any child had fever or any other problem he got all worried
> and came enquiring about them ten times a day, checking their
> temperature, giving them medicines.

Every Sunday he took the children for a long drive, singing, playing
pranks and cracking jokes all the way. Nephew Uday recalls that one
day, when Sanjeev was shooting at Century Bazaar for the film *Biwi
O Biwi*:

> He called me and my brother Prithvi over and bought us our
> favourite superhero costumes, bath towels and bed sheets.

There was even a day when he took both his nephews for a helicopter
ride during the shooting of *Sawaal*. According to his nephew Prithvi:

During Diwali, dada gave Uday and me hundred rupees as Diwali gift and we gave the money to Jamnadas to buy us firecrackers and at night we celebrated Diwali near our building.

Sanjeev was very careful about the children's education. He met the school principals in person and even took Jaya Bhaduri's help to get them enrolled in good schools. His nephew Uday recalls:

> He was so careful about our education that he personally saw our report cards and remarks. If he found that we were not up to the mark, he punished us. Punishment was not allowing us to watch TV or play video games. I learnt family values from dada; about how to give importance to family and work hard.

Sanjeev Kumar was also full of surprises. Although he usually insisted that his family use his cars and avoid public transport, one day, he gave in to his nephew's request and travelled in an autorickshaw with him while going out for lunch. His nephew Prithvi recalls,

> As we reached Hotel Gazebo at Hill Road, everyone was shocked to see top star Sanjeev Kumar in a rickshaw, but he never bothered about what others thought of him.

Sanjeev also treated Jamnadas's son, Deepak, like one of his own and took him along to visit Saibaba mandir with the rest of the Jariwala children.

*

Everyone who knew Sanjeev Kumar personally was well familiar with his love for good food. Gulzar recalled in an interview,

> Hari loved food. He loved eating non-vegetarian food and would tell my sister, who lived with me those days, 'I will come to have chicken.'

To me, he would say, 'I will come anytime. I need Black Label. If you cannot afford it, I will leave a bottle here with you.'

And, sure enough, he would drop in any time after a shoot, often without warning. And I would wake my sister up so she could cook something for him.

Every day after the shoot, when the unit would pack up, Sanjeev's party would begin. If legends are to be believed then Sanjeev, along with his friends, would go looking for dhabas after having finished his first round of dinner.

His friend Anju Mahendru was well acquainted with Sanjeev's constant hunt for good food:

Hari was a foodie. For him everything was about food. Despite being a Gujarati Brahmin, he loved non-vegetarian food. And unless it was at someone's home, he wasn't comfortable eating it. So he'd come home and we'd have dishes made for him. My mother [Shanti Mahendru, the late Madan Mohan's sister] also grew fond of him. She began tying a rakhi on him.

Moushumi Chatterjee, his co-star in *Angoor,* fondly recalls:

He used to treat me like a child. Sometimes he would come home when my husband and I were going out. He would say, 'You carry on . . . just tell your maid to cook some non-veg for me. Is there fish in the fridge?'

He would get film videos, watch them, eat, drink and leave. There were times he would come very late at night. I had just had Megha [her second daughter] then, and I would get very irritated. I would ask him, '*Yeh koi time hain aane ka? Aap yahan khana khane aata hai kya? Driver bhejdo, hum aapko dabba denge* (Is this any time to come? Do you come here to eat food? Send your driver, I will send you tiffin).'

Babu [Moushumi's husband, Jayanta] would feel so embarrassed. But Haribhai would tell him I'm like his mother.

His mother tried to rectify his eating and drinking habits initially but later gave up when they had already gone too far. However, she reminded him:

I don't want to hear anyone complain that my son drank so much that he embarrassed himself in the streets. So the best thing is to drink at home.

Sanjeev never smoked or drank in front of his mother out of respect.

One day Prem Chopra arranged for a get-together at his place, Nibbana, Pali Hill. The who's who of the Hindi film industry, including Sanjeev Kumar, were invited. It was 1 a.m. by the time the revellers left, and a tired Chopra finally retired to his bed. But suddenly, at around 2 a.m., someone rang the doorbell. Chopra rushed to open the door and found Sanjeev standing in front of him. Prem Chopra recalls:

'How can the party end without me?' he asked. I opened a bottle of wine for him and we both sat till six in the morning.

*

Sanjeev was a busy star, but he always remembered the people who helped him attain success and recognition. When his friend Chandravardhan Bhatt, who had introduced him into Gujarati theatre, requested him to perform two plays, *Niyayna Panth* and *Bahut Nachyo Gopal*, to commemorate his silver jubilee in Gujarati theatre, Sanjeev readily agreed without a second thought. Many film stars went to watch Sanjeev's performance on stage, including Amitabh Bachchan, Jaya Bachchan, Shatrughan Sinha, Asrani and even his arch rival, Rajesh Khanna. No one knew then that this was going to be Sanjeev Kumar's last performance. Niranjan Mehta recalls:

For those two shows, the tickets were four times more expensive but Sanjeev performed free of cost.

His sister-in-law Jyoti Jariwala remembers:

I went to see the play with my entire family and for the first time I saw his performance on stage as he had left theatre before my marriage.

In one of my interviews published in the Hindi weekly magazine *Movie Jagat*, in 1983, Sanjeev Kumar clarified why he didn't produce movies even though he had mentioned that he would eventually get into production. He said:

Today, to make a film is a very difficult task. I can't run after actors for their dates. I've seen how immensely complicated this whole process is. My suggestion to you is that if you have an enemy and you wish to seek revenge, encourage that person to be a film-maker or a politician. Both the fields are enough to ruin a person.

Sanjeev Kumar extended his support to all his friends in need and lent them money or became a part of their venture pro bono to help them succeed. His friend Girish Vaidya, who became the chief producer of the Films Division, needed funds for an ad film. He got in touch with Mahesh Desai, but unfortunately Mahesh Desai was going through a financial crunch, so he directed Vaidya to Sanjeev Kumar. Sanjeev readily agreed to help him out. He loaned Rs 35,000 without charging any interest. Vaidya, who had agreed to return the sum within two months, was ready to pay him back within forty-five days and when he reached Sanjeev's house to repay the loan, Sanjeev asked Vaidya to hand the money over to his mother since he was just about to leave for a shoot. Mahesh Desai recalls:

> As I gave the money to Shantaben, she told me many people took money from Hari, but only few people paid back.

There were rumours, however, that Sanjeev was a *kanjoos* and if sources are to be believed, it was a rumour Sanjeev encouraged. There came a time in his life when he would suspect everyone of trying to befriend him because of his money, leading to deep-seated trust issues. Whenever someone tried to get close to him, a couple of his friends would plant an idea into his mind saying that the girl in question wasn't in love with him but was only attracted to his money, and that would be enough for Sanjeev to back out of any relationship.

However, Sanjeev Kumar was philanthropic by nature, and he never shied away from his responsibilities. Those who know him will count instances such as the time when he arranged free stage shows to collect money for a fixed deposit made in the name of his bereaved friend Dilip Dutt's son, and when he inaugurated the restaurant and tailoring shop of his stylist Rohidas Bangera, free of cost. Rohidas Bangera, also known as Kiran, says:

> He was so helpful that before he came to inaugurate, he went to Shiv Sena leader Pramod Navalkar's place and brought him along with him.

There are many who'll comment on how Sanjeev was always late on sets but ask Vishal Desai, who was known as Master Bittu when he worked as a child artiste with Sanjeev Kumar in *Mukti* (1977), and he'll recall how Sanjeev made it a point to come early so that Vishal didn't miss his exams. One day, a show was organized, where all leading child artistes had to perform. Desai fondly remembers:

Sanjeev Kumar and Gulzar made a great actor–director combination, with *Aandhi* being the crowning glory of their collaboration

Another memorable Sanjeev Kumar–Gulzar collaboration, *Angoor*, a film that gave a great glimpse into the comic potential of the actor

One of the finest of the Gulzar–Sanjeev Kumar collaborations, *Namkeen*; Sanjeev Kumar made his presence felt in this film, which was largely driven by its women protagonists

One of the highlights of Sanjeev Kumar's acting career, *Dastak*, a film that fetched him numerous accolades

A big hit of its time, *Dharti Kahe Pukar Ke*

As the emotionally scarred protagonist, Sanjeev Kumar was brilliant in *Khilona*, a film that cemented his reputation as one of the finest actors of the era

Manoranjan, directed by Shammi Kapoor and based on Billy Wilder's *Irma la Douce*, was a film ahead of its time, with a typically robust Sanjeev Kumar performance

Providing yet another glimpse of the actor's range, *Nauker* gave Sanjeev Kumar the opportunity to display both his comic and dramatic potential

It is said that a taxi driver, responding to a film-maker's question about Sanjeev Kumar's pot belly in the song 'Thande Thande Paani Se' in *Pati Patni Aur Woh*, commented, 'When you watch Sanjeev Kumar, you forget his body . . . everything but his presence becomes immaterial'—another of the actor's celebrated performances

Sanjeev Kumar was the perfect foil to Hema Malini's star-making turn in *Seeta Aur Geeta*, which also starred Dharmendra; the song 'O Saathi Chal', featuring the actor in skates, remains evergreen

Mainstream Hindi cinema can be divided into two eras—before and after *Sholay*; the actor's performance as Thakur remains a perennial favourite and as iconic as Amjad Khan's Gabbar Singh

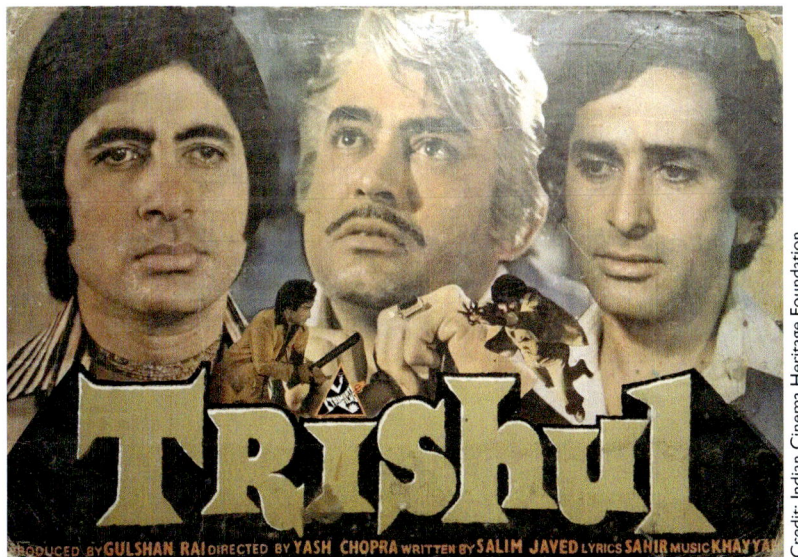

In keeping with his belief that the age of a character did not matter, only the role did, Sanjeev Kumar played Amitabh Bachchan's father in *Trishul*, a big hit of its time

Vidhata was another multistarrer where Sanjeev Kumar shone through despite the presence of Dilip Kumar and Shammi Kapoor

The actor starred in a number of 'social' melodramas in the 1970s; in *Yehi Hai Zindagi* he was once again cast in an elderly role as the patriarch of a family

Sanjeev uncle was the chief guest. After watching a few performances he decided to leave. My performance was right in the end so when I came to know that he was leaving I went to him and requested him to stay till my turn came and he agreed, he was there till the end of the show.

Another day, during the making of the film *Rahee* (1987), Sanjeev declared after the pack-up that he would be on the set by 9.30 a.m. on the following day. Shatrughan Sinha's brother, Dr Lakhan Sinha, who was producing the film, didn't believe him and a bet of Rs 100 was made between the two. The next day, Sanjeev won the bet after coming on time and then instructed Raman Kumar, the film's director, to make sure no one called him for the shoot before noon. Sinha, who had just lost the bet, was shocked. Sanjeev replied cheekily:

Our bet was to see if I come on time, not for me to begin shooting that early.

Everyone laughed at Sanjeev's wit. He was of course joking, and the shooting began as planned.

Another time, while shooting for *Namkeen*, Sanjeev was so late that Gulzar declared pack-up as soon as he arrived, saying:

I don't want to shoot any more.

Sanjeev addressed Jamnadas, saying:

Let us go for a movie. Hope Gulzar Sahib will also join us.

Gulzar laughed with the entire unit and the shooting began. Gulzar reminisces:

Hari and Pancham were my anchors; they were an integral part of my films. If they refused a part or were busy elsewhere, only then did I think of casting others. My commitment with Hari was such that I made sure the film ended with Hari's scene. I miss both of them so I stopped making films.

Sanjeev treated his colleagues like he would his own family. According to Parikshit Sahni:

> The day my father Balraj Sahni died, Sanjeev was by my side. If he had not been there, I would have killed myself. Crying, I put my head on his shoulder and he said, 'Today I lost my father for the second time.'

Producer–director Deepak Balraj Vij was the fourth assistant director to Shyam Ralhan in *Chowkidaar*. He was so new to the film industry that he didn't even know how to use a clapperboard correctly. It so happened that Sanjeev was all set for a close-up shot when Vij clapped the clapperboard so close to his face that chalk dust flew into Sanjeev's eyes, hindering his dialogue delivery. The director yelled 'cut!' and gave Vij a piece of his mind in front of everyone, but Sanjeev intervened, asked the director to calm down and taught Vij how to use a clapperboard. Deepak Balraj Vij remembers:

> And on my first day in the industry I learnt my first lesson from Sanjeev Kumar.

When Deepak became a successful producer–director, he decided to make a film, *Ghabrahat*, with Sanjeev, but the film could not go on to the floor because Sanjeev wasn't keeping well. Deepak says:

> But still the subject stayed with me as there was no alternative to Sanjeev Kumar.

His friends, as well as his acquaintances and people who worked for him, will never forget his generosity. He presented a flat to his secretary, Jamnadas, at Ambedkar Road, Pali Hill, a car to his friend Subhash Indori, and he even helped his chauffer, Subhash Dutta, get married and settle down.

According to his domestic help, Pandit, who is still working for the Jariwala family:

> Everyone was equal for him. Many times he took me along for dinners in five-star restaurants and I accompanied him in flights too. I never felt that he was my boss.

Sanjeev was very close to actress Sarika, who started working with him as a child artiste and then went on to play his son, granddaughter, lover and wife. Sarika laments:

> When I was pregnant with Shruti, we both spoke on the phone and he said, 'After delivery, when you come to Bombay with your newborn, inform me in advance so that I can take special permission from the airport authority and welcome you and your child inside the flight. I want your baby in my arms, before you put your foot on the land.'
> Unfortunately, he died before I came to Bombay.

When Sarika landed in Bombay for the first time with Shruti, she felt so bad at the airport that she broke down.

Although Sanjeev Kumar never got married, he had complete faith in the institution of marriage; and that's why he didn't step back from doing his bit to bring about a truce between Shatrughan Sinha and his wife, Poonam. According to reliable sources there were major problems between Shatrughan Sinha and Poonam Sinha and, at one point, things got so bad that they were not even on talking terms. When Sanjeev came to know about this, he sat down with them and sorted out their differences. Poonam Sinha was ever grateful to him and treated him like her own brother thereafter. History repeated itself when superstar Amitabh Bachchan and his wife, Jaya Bhaduri, were going through a difficult phase because of Bachchan's alleged romantic involvement with another famous actress. Jaya, who treated Sanjeev like a brother, was relieved when he stepped in to resolve their marital discord and saved their family from falling apart.

His sister-in-law Jyoti Jariwala asserts:

> Bhai was a family man, he felt that every wife and husband should be faithful and committed to each other.

The Jariwala family was very close to Tarla Joshi. When Tarla's husband, Pravin Joshi, got involved with actress Sarita Khatau, Sanjeev felt terrible for Tarla and held Sarita Khatau responsible for destroying Tarla's married life. Tarla Joshi recalls:

> Yes, when Pravin married Sarita, Baa [Shantaben] and Hari both felt bad for me. I was jobless. Hari told me that he will try to get me roles in films. But I refused it.

Pravin's brother Arvind Joshi also confirmed the same. When I approached Sarita Joshi to cooperate with me for this book, she refused to talk about Sanjeev Kumar.

*

Even after all these years, anecdotes from people who partook of Sanjeev's benevolence keep surfacing time and again. Like how he didn't charge a fee for shooting *Nauker* because the director had an untimely death and his widow couldn't gather enough money; like how he helped his mentor P.D. Shenoy by loaning him money in the early 1980s, when his Odia film was not progressing as planned; like how he sent B.R. Ishara Rs 20,000 through Jamnadas for *Log Kya Kahenge* when the film was almost on the verge of getting shelved. According to B.R. Ishara:

And you will be surprised to know that not only did he help me with twenty thousand rupees but he also refused to accept his instalment which was due. There was no buyer for the film but on his request distributor Gulshan Rai agreed to release my film.

Producer–director Govind Saraiya needed a lab letter (the industry equivalent of a no-objection certificate) from Sanjeev Kumar to approach other distributors, since his film *Priya* was not doing well in the NCR territory. No actor would give their lab letter unless their balance amount was cleared. Sanjeev's balance—Rs 60,000—was pending but Govind Saraiya wasn't in a position to borrow money from moneylenders and pay Sanjeev Kumar's due. According to Govind Saraiya:

> But without asking for the balance Sanjeev agreed to sign the lab letter and because of him I could release *Priya* in Bombay circuit. It was a flop but I recovered some of the amount so I decided to pay half his balance—thirty thousand rupees. I went to his place with my wife and while giving him the money I said, 'Sorry sir, please accept thirty thousand rupees because I cannot pay you the full amount.'
>
> He told me that I was the first producer who paid him at least half the amount after the film had flopped. When I was home with my wife, I was surprised to see her handing me back the same thirty thousand rupees which I had given Sanjeev. She told me that he had quietly given it back to her and asked her to keep it a secret. Actually he was aware about my financial crisis.

While narrating this incident he could not hold back tears and added:

> I have spent more than six decades in this industry and haven't met a single person worthy of being compared to Sanjeev Kumar. He was a great friend who understood the problems of his nearest and dearest people well.

According to producer–director J. Om Prakash:

> To be a good actor and to be a good human being are two different
> qualities and it is difficult to find both qualities in one man. In my
> entire career I found these two qualities only in Sanjeev Kumar.

During the making of *Hum Paanch*, producer Boney Kapoor needed
funds to complete his film and he was trying to acquire a loan from
various sources. When Sanjeev got to know about it, he came forward
and solved his problem by giving him the required amount, which
supposedly ran into lakhs. Jyoti Jariwala confirms this:

> We were not aware about the transaction between Bhai and Boney
> Kapoor. After Bhai's death suddenly one evening Boney came to
> our place with a big amount and that's when we came to know. It
> was Boney's greatness that he returned the money.

Even Raj Kapoor borrowed a couple of lakhs from Sanjeev to
complete his film *Biwi O Biwi,* but Kapoor could not pay back the
entire amount to Sanjeev. Jyoti Jariwala said:

> I needed money so Jamnadas-ji took me to Raj Kapoor. He paid
> some of the amount and the rest I had to forgo.

Sadly, there were many who didn't hesitate to take advantage of
Sanjeev's generosity. Apart from Raj Kapoor, there were many who
didn't bother returning his money. His partner Amar Lulla took a
loan from the bank on their property, Hotel Princess in Bangalore,
without informing him and showed heavy losses in their business.
After Sanjeev's death the family had to settle with Amar Lulla and
ended up selling their share for next to nothing. Sanjeev invested
lakhs in a pickle business with the lady who owned Aram Hotel near
the Mahim bus depot because she treated him kindly and earned his

trust. But ever since the day he passed away, she never showed her face to the family. According to Jyoti Jariwala:

> After Bhai's death many turned their faces and we came to know who his real friend was and who was not.

His nephew Uday Jariwala confirms:

> He helped a lot of actresses with their personal problems and helped them financially too, they used to call him Bhai.

Director Ravi Tandon was of this opinion:

> That was the problem. He used to sit with *tapori* people in the evening and trust everyone, I felt bad for him. But today I realize that he was a genius who treated all equally.

*

One day, Sanjeev was hurrying for a shoot but just as he was about to step out, Jamnadas stopped him in his tracks to point out that his kurta was burnt at the back owing to careless ironing. Apprehensive about the star's image, Jamnadas requested him to change, but Sanjeev, being his modest self, calmly stated:

> Let it be. I don't care what people think about me. I have to reach the set on time as the producers are facing a crisis and the time I waste to change can cost them lakhs of rupees. If a person judges you by your clothes, that person should be asked what was he wearing when he came into this world.

Sanjeev Kumar did a lot of charity without beating his own drum publicly. According to Jayshree T.:

Yes, I have witnessed his charity. If he helped someone he never spoke about it to another person, not even to his family.

After Sanjeev's death, Jamnadas produced a list of people who had taken a loan from him, and the Jariwala family was shocked at the length of the list and the huge sum total of the loans. In the mid-1980s, he had lent a staggering Rs 94,36,000, which even today is a vast sum of money. The family tried to recover the amount from Sanjeev's friends, but the response was not good. At last, they approached Sunil Dutt with Jamnadas, as Dutt was a very respectable man in the film industry and people, more often than not, did his bidding. Dutt was shocked to see the list and the names of all the eminent producers, directors and actors it contained. But Dutt was frank and told the family:

> Sanjeev was innocent and all these people had taken advantage of him. Now that he has passed away it would be near impossible to recover the money. But nevertheless I will try my best.

According to Deepak, Jamnadas's son:

> But in a few days we came to know that Dutt Sahab had also failed to recover Sanjeev Uncle's money.

Sanjeev Kumar came into this world empty-handed but left behind limitless empathy and compassion in his wake.

18

Life After the Heart Attacks

Unbeknownst to most, Sanjeev Kumar, like his father and brothers, had a congenital heart condition; this condition was why the male members of his family seldom lived beyond fifty. Most of his life, he enjoyed good health, and the occasional illness was treated with Shantaben's ayurvedic medicines or home-made wellness formulae. Apart from the medicated tooth powder prescribed by Dr Chandiwala, Sanjeev was not on any medication and, given how spirited and vivacious he was, no one could have guessed that at thirty-seven, the peak of his career, he would experience his first heart attack.

This was in 1976. His family members rushed him to Nanavati Hospital fearing the worst. This incident wasn't publicized because he was involved in many high-budget projects, like *Imaan Dharam*, *Zindagi*, *Mukti*, *Paapi* and *Yahi Hai Zindagi*. B.R. Ishara said:

> I was supposed to shoot with him for *Log Kya Kahenge*. When he didn't turn up, I tried to contact him. Jamnadas informed me that he had left for Ahmedabad and I had to cancel my shoot. Later, I found out that he had been hospitalized.

This news, however, could not be hidden for long and, as word spread, thousands of people made a beeline for Nanavati Hospital, showing their support and praying for his speedy recovery. Many well-known names from the industry visited him at the hospital, including director Raj Tilak, Sunil Dutt, Rajendra Kumar, Sharmila Tagore, Sachin and A.K. Hangal. Director Govind Saraiya was a regular visitor as his film *Angaarey* was on the set. Misunderstandings cropped up when Subhash Indori and Johnny Whisky refused to permit Gulzar, Prem Chopra, Geeta Siddharth and others to see him. Prem Chopra later clarified:

> When Sanjeev found out, he called and apologized on behalf of his friends and I went to see him again.

Shantaben and Nikul were by his side day in and day out, nursing him back to health. Each morning, his mother would arrive at Nanavati Hospital with a packet of food and a bottle of water, and sit beside his bed until Nikul arrived in the evening and took over.

After Sanjeev Kumar was discharged from the hospital, he went to director Ravi Tandon's home at Tandon House, Juhu, since his own bedroom in Parin Villa was on the second floor and he had been asked to avoid staircases. Dr Gandhi, whose clinic was nearby, visited him every day. His mother, brother, Jamnadas and nephews as well as friends, like Subhash Indori, Dilip Dutt and Johnny Whisky, were regular visitors. Ravi Tandon recalls:

> I had given him my own bedroom with the balcony overlooking the sea, and shifted into the dining room with my wife. His food was provided by his family as per the doctor's instruction. At night, without informing his family, he used to send Jamnadas or his driver to bring non-veg food from a five-star restaurant. He used to enjoy playing with my children Raj and Raveena.

However, the stay was short-lived because Sanjeev, desperate to find some respite from all the visitors, escaped to a hotel in Pune.

Sanjeev would wear a Nepali topi or a Dhaka topi to cover his head because it had to be shaved for his treatment. When his hair grew back, he gave the topi to his friend Sachin. Because of his heart attack, *Mukti's* schedule had suffered. However, he wasted no time post his brief hiatus to get back on the floors. An emotional scene was to be picturized on him but had to be altered since his doctor had advised him to avoid emotional situations.

Ashok Kumar was very particular about his health. He practised homeopathy as a hobby, and when he found out about a seminar on the topic of heart disease, he asked Sanjeev to attend. One of the doctors, talking about helping patients during a heart attack, said that the best person to take one's care in such a situation was one's spouse. They listened to the seminar with rapt attention and, afterwards, Ashok Kumar reminded Sanjeev about the doctor's advice:

Your marriage is more important than your career now. You need someone to share your life with.

Sanjeev replied,

Sir, after the attack, I have become more mature and I can take care of my health on my own.

Sanjeev Kumar didn't take his heart disease seriously enough. On 6 October 1976, he left for Canada with B.R. Chopra and Vidya Sinha to attend a film festival, knowing full well that it was harmful for him to take long flights. One day, he was attending a get-together when he suddenly complained of discomfort. He was rushed to the nearest hospital, the Breach Candy Hospital. This time as well, there were attempts to hush this piece of news from the film industry. He was hospitalized for a few days. This wasn't a heart attack, but the Jariwala family took this very seriously and all the medical check-ups were done under actor–director Deven Verma's brother-in-law Dr Hiren Seth's supervision.

In May 1978, he went to the USA to attend stage shows and spend time with his sister Gayatri, who was expecting her second child. At around 5 p.m. on 12 June 1978, Gayatri went into labour, and Sanjeev rushed her to the Brazoria Community Hospital, informing her husband Ashok Patel, who was away. After Ashok arrived at the hospital, Sanjeev returned to Gayatri's house, where her friends Kapila and Jayant were staying to keep him company. Next morning, at around 7.30 a.m., Gayatri gave birth to a girl. Elated by the news, Sanjeev and Jayant decided to go shopping for the little one. Before they could step out, however, Sanjeev suffered a second heart attack and collapsed right before Kapila's and Jayant's eyes. Shocked, the couple called an ambulance, got Sanjeev admitted and informed Ashok. Leaving his clueless wife and new-born baby behind, Ashok went to visit Sanjeev at the Methodist Hospital.

After almost three days had passed with no sign of Sanjeev, Gayatri began to get suspicious. She couldn't believe that he wouldn't come to meet his niece. Ashok tried to convince her that he had come while she was fast asleep and that he was busy with Sunil Dutt, who also happened to be in the States, but Gayatri knew that something was being kept from her.

In India, Jamnadas too had a hunch that all was not well with his friend. It was very unlike Sanjeev to not call home for so long and personally share Gayatri's wonderful news. Jamnadas decided to call Gayatri the day she was discharged from the hospital and ask her what the matter was. When Gayatri received Jamnadas's call she told him that Bhai probably hadn't called them for so long because he was busy with Sunil Dutt. This information confirmed Jamnadas's suspicions because he had met Sunil Dutt on the previous day. He decided not to upset Gayatri and chose to raise the issue with Ashok instead. Ashok caved in and told him the truth about Sanjeev's health.

Jamnadas received this dreadful news and the entire Jariwala household went into shock. His nephew Prithvi's first birthday party had to be cancelled, and when Gayatri found out, she left her infant at home to take care of her brother at the hospital. He was in the hospital for fifteen days and Gayatri remained by his side, talking to the doctors and doing the needful. The doctors had put several restrictions on Sanjeev's lifestyle, but all warnings fell on deaf ears because as soon as he started recovering, throwing caution to the winds, he reverted to his old habits.

One day, when Ashok went to visit Sanjeev, he noticed that the room smelt of cigarettes. Astonished at how careless one could be, Ashok confronted Sanjeev, who staunchly denied that he had smoked. Ashok wouldn't let the matter rest. He spotted a box of cigarettes lodged under his mattress, and when he asked him how on earth he had managed to procure cigarettes inside the hospital, he learnt that Sanjeev had convinced a nurse, who was his fan, to smuggle a cigarette packet into his room. Ashok approached the nurse and asked her if she was ready to face the consequences of this act. She replied:

> I decided if something went wrong, I would readily to go to jail for him.

Before leaving the US, Sanjeev finally took his niece into his arms and named her Artee. Years later, Artee would be crowned Miss India Texas 2001 and would follow in her uncle's footsteps, acting in movies like *American Addiction* (2003), *Dancing in Twilight* (2005) and *Love and Marry* (2007). She recalled:

> I was hardly seven years old when my Mama [Sanjeev Kumar] passed away. I still remember him very well.

In October 1984, while shooting for *Professor Ki Padosan* (1993), Sanjeev Kumar once again complained of feeling uncomfortable. Jamnadas promptly informed the producer of Sanjeev's condition and they all agreed that Sanjeev should stay at home and rest. Sanjeev, however, reached the studios to resume shooting the minute he felt better, assuring everyone that he would visit the hospital for a routine check-up right after pack-up. He completed his shot on a two-wheeler with Padmini Kolhapure and left for Nanavati Hospital. His enthusiasm and zeal to continue normal life did not fool the doctors and they kept him under observation that night. Upon returning home, he started keeping a bell with him to summon his attendants instead of shouting their names. After resting at home for a few more days he resumed his work once again in November.

On the night of 20 December 1984, he woke up clutching the left side of his chest. The pain was so severe that, first thing the next morning, he only washed his face and left for Nanavati Hospital without informing anyone. As soon as he stepped out of his car, he had to ask for a wheelchair and oxygen. The doctors asked him to have an immediate bypass surgery. He spent five days recuperating in the hospital and, the moment he got discharged, he rushed to meet his producers. According to director Raman Kumar:

> It was his greatness that he called his producers before deciding on his heart surgery, to discuss their projects.

He also discussed his surgery with his family, and everyone decided that he should opt for an open-heart surgery in the US. He called his chartered accountant and lawyer and drafted a will that no one was aware of at the time. He made it amply clear that they were to declare his will only in the event of his death.

In the last week of February 1985, he left for the US, refusing to let anyone from his family accompany him. Only his friend Hari Walia's son, Ravi Walia, went with him. He didn't even allow his family to see him off at the airport because he didn't want to break down in front of them. He bade farewell to each one, barring Uday, who was in boarding school, and left for the airport.

His bypass was fixed for the second week of March 1985 at Saint Luke Hospital, Houston, to be performed by a well-known heart

surgeon, Dr Dintal Kuli. The legend goes that, at seventy, Dr Kuli
would operate on five heart patients in quick succession in the
same operating theatre, moving from one surgery to the next, as his
assistants stitched up the previous patient. Coincidentally, Nikul was
also supposed to be operated on by the same doctor. Sanjeev Kumar's
sister-in-law Jyoti Jariwala recalls:

> We ensured with Dr Kuli that Bhai's operation would take place
> first, we wanted to avoid the risk of the doctor growing exhausted
> after a couple of operations.

On the day, Sanjeev left for the hospital with Gayatri and Ravi Walia
at 5 a.m., on an empty stomach as instructed. The operation was to
take place at 7.30 a.m. Two ward boys dutifully arrived at 7 a.m. to
prep him for the operation—they helped him change into a hospital
gown and asked him to lie down on a stretcher. As he was wheeled
towards the operating theatre, he tried to disguise his nervousness, but
his sister could sense his fear. Before entering the operating theatre, he
smiled at his sister, but his eyes filled with tears. Gayatri mustered all
her courage and assured him that everything would be all right.

At exactly 7.35 a.m., the green bulb above the operating theatre
door was switched on. Gayatri, eyes fixated on the bulb and constantly
checking the time, fervently prayed for her brother's safety. Every
moment seemed like an eternity. It was almost 2 p.m. before the
light was switched off, and the doctor's assistant informed Gayatri
that Sanjeev's surgery was successful and that he would be shifted
to his room by 4 p.m. Immensely relieved as she was, Gayatri still
refused to touch a morsel of food or drink a drop of water until she
saw her brother for herself. Sanjeev was unconscious for twenty-two
hours. When he opened his eyes for the first time, he found Gayatri
there by his bedside. He was in no position to talk, but he was clearly
worried about her. In those days, patients had to stay in the hospital
for at least three weeks after a heart surgery, and it was the first week
of April by the time he was discharged.

Jyoti, her children and Tarla Joshi came to the US at the end of April to see Sanjeev, and he was delighted to meet his nephews and niece. His friend and co-star Shatrughan Sinha, who happened to be in the US, flew to Houston to check on his friend's health.

Gayatri took care of his diet for the next three months. She cooked vegetarian dishes like daal, kadi and sabzi with no salt, as the doctor had instructed. He lost a lot of weight and steadily grew weaker. The producers kept calling, reminding him of his pending work and worrying him. R.K. Nayyar and Sadhana Nayyar would call him every alternate day. Having fully recovered and having spent quality time with his family and friends in the US, Sanjeev returned to India.

Back home, he made the lifestyle changes his doctors had suggested and ate home-cooked food with less salt. He woke up at seven in the morning, walked at home, stayed at home, watched television in the evening and went to bed by ten at night. He stopped going for film parties and his drinking buddies kept away from him.

In August 1985, producer–director R.K. Nayyar threw a welcome party for him at the Hotel Sun-n-Sand in Juhu Chowpatty. The media was invited by party publicist Harish Mehra.

A banner declaring 'Welcome Home, Sanjeev Kumar!' was strung up over the entrance; Sunil Dutt and Marc Zuber were the first ones to arrive. At around 9.30 p.m., Sanjeev Kumar entered wearing a black tuxedo. He was happy, this was his first public appearance after his surgery, but everyone could see that he looked much frailer than before. Sunil Dutt hugged him and presented him with a bouquet, and everyone got busy with the revelries. At around 11.30 p.m., Prakash Mehra entered with Shatrughan Sinha and Poonam Sinha.

I went up to him to wish him a speedy recovery, and he responded with his ever-charming smile. The heart attacks and surgeries couldn't diminish the power of that smile. One never thought that this would be my last meeting with him, and perhaps Sanjeev Kumar never thought that this would be his last film party.

Within a short period of time, he picked up his under-production films again, but sheer willpower was no longer enough. He first shot R.K. Nayyar's *Qatl* (1986), followed by Nitin Manmohan's *Baat Ban Jaye* (1986) at Filmcity, Goregaon. Someone would hold his hand during shoots and support him while he carried a walking stick. Director Bharat Rangachary decided to take only long- and mid-shots of Sanjeev Kumar. Despite this the films were hardly progressing. He couldn't walk or deliver his dialogues properly. The crew, used to an eloquent Sanjeev Kumar, was astonished to see his lips moving silently. Many directors had to resort to dubbing Sanjeev's lines.

For director Raman Kumar's film *Rahee* (1987), Sanjeev was required to sit down and immediately rise to deliver his lines. As the camera rolled, Sanjeev sat down but could not manage to stand up on time. After many failed attempts, Raman Kumar decided to let him stand and say his lines.

The climax scene in M.N. Yasin's *Kanch Ki Deewar* (1986) had Amrish Puri being hit by a bullet and falling on to Sanjeev's lap before breathing his last. During the shoot, as Sanjeev bent to catch Puri, he lost his balance and broke his knees. Later, the scene was completed with Sanjeev wearing pads on his knees; such was his devotion to his craft.

Despite all these health problems, not once did Sanjeev discontinue his shoot. He had struggled to enter this industry and he was struggling when he was on the verge of leaving it all behind. He battled his circumstances as he always had. His only focus was on completing the ongoing projects. A man of his word, he didn't want his producers to suffer because of him.

However, the more he faced the camera, the more he realized that he was not the same person any more. His body was failing him, although his spirit pushed him forward. A mere shadow of his former self, a spectre of the star he used to be, he knew he was counting his days and he saw the futility in denying himself the little pleasures that life still held in store for him. The more he tried, the more he suffered; and, one day, he decided that he had had enough.

After almost fourteen months of being a teetotaller, he gave in to the temptation of opening a bottle of wine.

Jamnadas tried to politely remind him that the doctors had forbidden alcohol. On the third day, when Sanjeev still wouldn't budge, Jamnadas held his hand and stopped him from taking a sip, saying,

Today I won't allow you to drink this, you have to stop!

Livid, Sanjeev retorted,

Who are you to stop me?

The argument escalated, with Jamnadas and Sanjeev tugging at the glass until it slipped from Sanjeev's grasp and shattered into pieces on the floor. This was the first time they had fought and, enraged, Sanjeev fired Jamnadas on the spot.

Jamnadas had never foreseen this black day, not even in his nightmares; he had never imagined that one day their friendship would come to this. There was no one to intervene and he left Sanjeev's house in silence. Jamnadas's son, Deepak, recalled that night:

My father was honest to Sanjeev Uncle and his family. He never felt like an outsider. He was there at every stage, the ups and downs. He never used Sanjeev uncle's name for his benefit, like making a film with him and becoming a reputed producer as the other stars' secretaries had done. Till Sanjeev Uncle's last breath, he worked only for him. Sanjeev Uncle loved him and treated him like his own family member. Later, he worked for Pratibha Sinha, Kumar Sanu, Poonam Dhillon and Sadashiv Amrapurkar. But the day my father fought with Sanjeev Uncle, that day was a black day for both the families.

Sanjeev Kumar hadn't anticipated that his blunder would cost him such a dear friendship. Who knew him like Jamnadas did?

After Jamnadas left, he was truly alone and facing hardships from all quarters. He couldn't bear his isolation, so he moved into his friend Raj Kumar's bungalow at Janki Kutir, Juhu. Raj Kumar was a Dubai-based businessman and Sanjeev's best friend.

During this time, Sanjeev had become a recluse and had distanced himself from his colleagues. One day, producer Kant Kumar received a call from Sanjeev asking him to meet him at Raj Kumar's bungalow. Sanjeev was all by himself, immersed in a book. He offered him a seat and said:

> There is a good report about your film in the industry. I called you to discuss this pending project. I request you to complete *Professor Ki Padosan* as soon as possible with me as I am planning a long holiday.

In a 1994 interview published in the Hindi weekly magazine *Filmcity*, Kant Kumar recalled:

> He was visibly disturbed. I could read the sadness on his face.

Sanjeev told Kant Kumar about his argument with Jamnadas, and how handicapped he was without his former secretary by his side. He asked Kumar to publish the fact that Jamnadas no longer worked for him in the trade magazines (*Trade Guide*, *Film Information*), in such a way that Jamnadas's feelings wouldn't be hurt. People were understandably taken aback when they found out.

Particularly infuriated, Tarla Joshi contacted Jamnadas and said accusingly:

> 'You should at least have informed me before leaving Hari. How can you do this?' When he told me what had transpired, I immediately confronted Sanjeev and he said, 'Whom should I live for now? I don't want to live. I want to die. Everything is over in my life.' I cooled him down and reminded him of

his nephews and niece. He broke down and asked me to call Jamnadas back.

The very next day Jamnadas was back in Parin Villa, by Sanjeev's side. They were meeting after fifteen days, but it seemed like they were meeting after years. They hugged and cried and begged for each other's forgiveness. It was truly wonderful that they had patched things up since Sanjeev had just fifteen days left to live.

19

The Final Farewell

One can only imagine the demons Sanjeev Kumar had to battle in his last days: the loneliness, the powerlessness and constant struggle with bitter hopelessness. He had wrung every drop of life from the fabric of his existence; battled against his circumstances and done his best. He was the master of his fate. Even with just a few precious days left, far from accepting defeat, he kept moving forward, determined to complete what he had started. Film director Raman Kumar recounts,

> He advised me to complete his dubbing for *Rahee*. I was not ready but he forced me, I did as he said, and, within a couple of days he passed away.

Jyoti had planned a long trip to Calcutta and Banaras with her family. She left Parin Villa on 29 October 1985 with all her children except Uday, who stayed back because he wanted to spend some time with his dada. He spent four days at home with his uncle and, on 3 November, left for Calcutta to join his mother. Jyoti Jariwala recalls:

We decided to visit the holy city of Banaras to pray for Bhai and the family, because for quite a while we had all been getting this premonition that something bad was about to happen.

On 28 October, Sanjeev spoke to his sister Gayatri for the last time, and the phone call lasted for more than thirty minutes. Recalling their last conversation, Gayatri couldn't hold back tears:

> He was so emotional; he advised me to take care of my health and my family. He told me not to depend on others, since no one knows when the time will come to face the world all alone. At that time, I didn't understand what he wanted to say.

Dinesh Hingoo, Sanjeev's friend and co-star, was about to leave for Muscat but he had a gut feeling about meeting Sanjeev:

> Before going to Muscat with Amjad Khan and Kalyanji–Anandji, I had a feeling that I must meet Sanjeev personally. My soul forced me to see him, for two days after I reached Muscat, he was no more.

Sanjeev spent the entire day of 5 November dubbing for R.K. Nayyar's *Qatl* at Sumit Dubbing Theatre, Juhu. He met Prakash Mehra and discussed his film *Insaan Ki Aulaad*. It was 10.30 p.m. by the time he finished dubbing; his last line was:

> *Qabr ke sirane kabhi ghans nahi ugti, barkhurdar* (grass doesn't grow near a headstone).

Leaving the dubbing theatre, he said to R.K. Nayyar:

> Tomorrow is my mother's death anniversary, so I will stay at home.

He was supposed to leave for London on 7 November 1985; and 6 November 1985 arrived with a tinge of sadness. Sanjeev was lost in his thoughts, reminiscing about the days of his childhood, thinking about his mother, longing for the feel of her fingers running through his hair. He was up at 7 a.m. but felt no urge to eat. Pandit, who had worked for him since 1968, kept insisting that he shouldn't starve and, after a lot of coaxing, was able to make Sanjeev take a sip of tea with some biscuits. The day brightened up momentarily when his mentor P.D. Shenoy came to return some money and Subhash Ghai dropped by to check on him. He sat and chatted with Ghai for a while.

After Ghai left, Sanjeev discussed how things would be when he left for London and offered Pandit Rs 2000 to see them through his absence, but Pandit refused the money since he already had enough. Hardly was the conversation over when Sanjeev complained of feeling nauseous. At about 12.30 p.m., Sanjeev vomited and an anxious Jamnadas made a frantic call to Dr Gandhi, asking him to come at once.

Sanjeev kept insisting that he was all right, that it was nothing and that all he wanted was to take a bath and get dressed because he was expecting Sachin over at any moment. He went into his bedroom, while Jamnadas and Pandit waited anxiously for Dr Gandhi to arrive. Sachin arrived with director Satpal and Dr Gandhi soon followed. Sachin, Satpal, Jamnadas, Dr Gandhi and Pandit were all eagerly waiting for Sanjeev to emerge from his bedroom. It had been more than forty-five minutes and there was no sign of him. Seriously worried by now, they decided to go in and see if he was all right. They found the bedroom door unlocked. (Sanjeev had been instructed to not lock bedroom and bathroom doors in case of an emergency.) Sachin pushed the door open and loudly exclaimed, 'Oh my God!'

Sanjeev Kumar was lying on the floor, immobile. He looked so peaceful, he could have been asleep.

It was a Wednesday. According to the doctor, Sanjeev must have suffered a fatal heart attack trying to get up from the sofa to go to the bathroom. Since the exact time of his death was unknown, it was assumed to be sometime between 1.45 and 2 p.m. He was only forty-seven years old.

Jamnadas informed Jyoti's brother and he arranged for their tickets back home the very next morning, without telling them the entire truth. Jyoti only knew that Sanjeev had been hospitalized because his health had deteriorated.

His brother Kishore and sister-in-law Prafulla were alerted as well. Prafulla recalls:

Kishore was crying like a child.

Tarla Joshi took the responsibility of breaking this dreadful news to his sister Gayatri.

In Bombay, the entire film industry came to a standstill. All shooting, recording, dubbing, post-production work got cancelled. Everyone was calling each other to notify them about Sanjeev's passing. Kishore Kumar wept with grief and disbelief. Rajesh Khanna and Ravi Tandon were shooting for *Nazrana* and they cancelled the shoot in honour of Sanjeev Kumar. Sudhir Dalvi was shooting with the Ramsay Brothers for *Saya*. He too cancelled the shoot.

A.K. Hangal recalled mournfully:

I never cried even when I lost my own family. But I could not control my tears when I found out that Hari was no more. I was sitting at the dining table and before I could eat, an army officer informed me about Hari's death. I could not eat and I could not even shoot.

Amjad Khan was in Muscat when he found out about Sanjeev's death but he thought that it was just a rumour, so he asked his wife to go to Parin Villa and see how he was doing. Shaila Khan recalls:

When he [Amjad] called me, I was not aware about Sanjeev's
death. I visited Parin Villa. I found a huge crowd outside and I
understood what it meant. I went back home and called Amjad to
confirm that what he'd heard was in fact true.

Actor Dinesh Hingoo remembers the sad day:

While Amjad Khan was speaking to his wife, I was standing next
to him. Amjad cried like a lost child, and he was not in a position
to perform on stage.

This was confirmed by producer Vinay Sinha. Remembering Sanjeev,
Dilip Kumar said:

Sanjeev was a great actor and a great man; he could have
achieved so much more, but destiny didn't support him. He
never changed, I knew him since he was struggling. After taking
a course in acting, he worked with me and became successful,
but success never changed him. Weak people cannot digest their
success but he was strong.

His sister was on her way from the US, and it was decided that his
funeral would take place on 8 November, only after she arrived, so
his remains were placed in a glass coffin. Shatrughan Sinha stood
sentinel beside Sanjeev's coffin for two days. Sinha stated:

I know many people will speak a lot about him now because he
is not here to justify himself. I am not going to say how great an
actor he was or how the film industry is going to lose one of its
biggest assets because this is already a fact. His death is a personal
loss for me and it goes deeper than our film background. I have
lost a great friend. He was my best friend. I shared a great rapport
with him. During any crisis, when I needed him he was always
there for me, lending me his support. I am proud to call him

my friend. If I asked him what his last wish was, he would have said, 'I don't want to die.' After the death of his younger brother his responsibilities had increased drastically, especially towards Nikul's children. These three children meant everything to him, and he wished to live for their future.

Kant Kumar, producer of *Professor Ki Padosan* and a member of the Indian Motion Pictures Producers' Association (IMPPA) welfare trust, was at a Films Division office for some work at the time of Sanjeev's death. After he finished his work, he telephoned the IMPPA head office. Ramraj Nahta answered the phone and asked him to get to the office immediately.

In a 1994 interview for the Hindi weekly *Filmcity*, Kant Kumar recalled the incident:

> When I reached IMPPA office all the producers were sitting quietly and everyone looked sombre. I asked them what the matter was but nobody replied.

After Kumar had asked thrice, Ramraj Nahta replied:

> Sanjeev's condition is not good and we all are worried about him.

Kant Kumar immediately called home and when he was told the terrible truth, the telephone receiver slipped from his hand. Manmohan Desai came forward, held his hand and assured him:

> He is still alive, whatever you have heard is a rumour doing the rounds all morning.

Kant Kumar remembers:

> I could make out that they knew Sanjeev had died, but they were hiding it from me because they were all worried about how I

would react, considering I had invested a huge amount in Sanjeev's *Professor Ki Padosan*.

He called Parin Villa to confirm the news and when there was no doubt left, Kant Kumar wept hysterically. Desai consoled him as best he could, assuring him that they could all understand his devastation—the loss of a colleague as well as the loss of a key actor in his forthcoming movie:

We will help you start another film.

Kant Kumar managed to get a grip on his emotions and decided to pay Sanjeev his last homage at Parin Villa. When Kant Kumar beheld Sanjeev's mortal remains, his mind returned to his last meeting with Sanjeev, when he had said,

I request you to complete this film as soon as possible as I am going on a long holiday.

Dinesh Hingoo asserts:

He died due to his loneliness. If he were married he would have lived longer. His problem was he didn't take rest. Even after bypass surgery, he continued to work. Filmmakers were responsible for his death; they didn't allow him to take rest.

Jyoti, who was travelling to Bombay with her three kids, was clueless about what had happened to her brother-in-law, until Uday pointed to a newspaper that a co-passenger was reading. Sanjeev Kumar's photograph was on the front page along with the words 'Sanjeev Kumar is no more!' Uday was astounded:

I didn't believe it. I thought, how can he die? If his family didn't know how could this newspaper find out?

Jyoti read the front page and broke down on the flight. Anju Mahendru remembers:

> A few days back he had been shooting in the same studio as me. I could not recognize him. When I walked past him, he said, 'Hello! You forget me?' I recognize his voice. I was shocked to see him and that was the last time I met him.

Mard's premiere, on the verge of getting cancelled, was still going ahead on the evening of 7 November because a lot had already been invested in it. In order to commemorate the occasion, Sanjeev Kumar's garlanded photograph, sent by Jamnadas, was placed on centre stage.

Outside, a huge starstruck crowd had gathered to see the film stars who were coming for the premiere. Apart from the chief guest, Kona Prabhakar, the governor of Maharashtra, many film personalities were present, including Manmohan Desai, Ramraj Nahta, B.K. Adarsh, Amrita Singh, Amitabh Bachchan, Dara Singh, Bob Christo, Pranlal Mehta, Dada Kondke, Ruksana Sultan and Goga Kapoor. Niranjan Mehta and Amitabh Bachchan lit candles and placed them in front of Sanjeev's photograph, and then Amitabh Bachchan addressed the crowd:

> *Aaj jin paristhitiyon mein is film ka premier kiya jaa raha hai woh bahut hi dukhad hai. Guzre kal hi hamara priy abhineta aur mera ek achcha mitra Sanjeev Kumar hamein chhodkar chale gaye. Hari Bhai ke chale jaane se puri film industry apne aap mein ek khokhlapan mehsoos kar rahi hai. Aaiye hum sab apni jagah khade hokar do minute ka moun dhaaran karein aur bhagwan se prarthana karein ki Hari Bhai ka shokakul pariwar is haadse ko bardasht kar paaye.* (The circumstances in which this film is being premiered are truly tragic. Yesterday a great actor and my dear friend Sanjeev Kumar left us forever. Hari Bhai's departure has left the entire film industry feeling hollow. Come, let's stand and observe two minutes

of silence and pray to the Almighty, so Hari Bhai's bereaved family
is able to cope with this immense loss.)

In the early hours of 8 November 1985, Gayatri Patel landed in India
and, as soon as she arrived, everyone made arrangements to carry
Sanjeev Kumar's remains to the crematorium. Sanjeev's last journey
set off from Parin Villa at 10.20 a.m. His brother Kishore, maternal
uncle Govind Bhai, and his friends Sunil Dutt and Amitabh Bachchan
volunteered to carry his remains. The thousands of people who
had gathered to witness this sorrowful procession chanted 'Sanjeev
Kumar *amar rahein*' in unison. A truck decorated with flowers was
to bear Sanjeev Kumar's remains from Parin Villa to Juhu Garden
Crematorium, and a huge throng of people, including yours truly,
walked beside it. As this procession reached Khar junction, Jeetendra
emerged from his car and joined the crowd. Almost everyone from
the film fraternity was present that day.

When Sanjeev's funeral procession reached the crematorium,
we found more than 500 people who had been waiting there for
two hours to catch a last glimpse of their hero. The last rites were
performed by his thirteen-year-old nephew, Uday.

During the funeral proceedings, Kishore pointed to one of the
raised platforms and said to family friend Sudarshan Nag:

See these three platforms? My younger brother Nikul's last
rites were performed on the first platform and now my elder
brother Hari is on the third platform. I think I will be on the
middle platform.

'Exactly six months later, I was there to attend Kishore's funeral and
he was, indeed, on the middle platform,' recalled Sudarshan Nag.

Kishore Jariwala passed away on 5 May 1986 at Bhatia Hospital
Tardeo, due to severe breathing problems. At the time of his death,
Gayatri was in the US and his last rites were performed by Nikul's
second son, Prithvi. According to Jyoti Jariwala:

Kishore Bhai took good care of us. He used to inquire after our well-being daily. I lost two brothers in six months' time.

Eight days after Sanjeev's untimely death, his best friend, Raj Kumar, organized a prayer meeting at his bungalow Janki Kutir, where Sanjeev Kumar had spent his last days.

Strangely, the ones who were truly close to Sanjeev were not in town when he passed away. A.K. Hangal, Amjad Khan, Dinesh Hingoo, Vidya Sinha, Govind Saraiya, L.P. Prasad, none of them were in Bombay. Sarika, who had known him since her childhood, learnt about his death fifteen days after he passed away. She said:

> I was in the remote mountains of Tamil Nadu, a place people
> went for hunting, accompanying someone for a shoot. There were
> no telephones and newspaper facilities. I returned to this sad news.
> I was shocked. I never thought Hari would leave me like this.

People who played a crucial role in Sanjeev Kumar's life passed away within six months of his death, including Aspi Irani, who went missing on 20 November 1985 and was declared dead after a couple of years; Irani had introduced Sanjeev in his stunt films *Nishan* and *Badal*.

Writer Gulshan Nanda, whose *Khilona* had given Sanjeev his first taste of commercial success, passed away on 16 November 1985, exactly ten days after Sanjeev. Producer J.B.H. Wadia, whose stunt film *Nishan* had given Sanjeev an opportunity to play a double role, passed away on 4 January 1986, exactly two months after Sanjeev's passing.

The man who played the role of an old man on stage and on screen never got the chance to grow old. Such is the irony of life.

20

The Last Will and Testament

It took the Jariwala family a week to accept that Sanjeev Kumar was never coming back. They were picking up the pieces of their lives in a bid to move on, when their chartered accountant, Bhawaniya and Company, informed them of the will Sanjeev Kumar had made, seeking to protect his property and guarantee the welfare of his family. The existence of this will proves that Sanjeev had known that his end was near.

It was mutually decided that, in accordance with his wishes, the will would be read in the presence of all of Sanjeev's family and friends, including Tarla Joshi, Shatrughan Sinha and Jamnadas. Everyone gathered around and waited with bated breath as Bhawaniya took his time to arrange the documents. Finally, the moment of truth had arrived.

According to the extensive will, Jyoti, Uday and Prithvi would receive 30 per cent each of his property including his monetary and other assets. The remaining 10 per cent would go to his niece Ekta, who was hardly three years old at the time. However, there was a condition in Jyoti's share. She had to pay Rs 3000 every month to Prafulla, Kishore's wife, out of her share, and another Rs 3000 for every child Prafulla might bear. As Tarla Joshi says:

This was the security for his brother Kishore's family. See how he financially protected his entire family, who does this?

Sanjeev had even kept Rs 2 lakh aside in his will for Jamnadas's son Deepak's education. However, strangely enough, nothing was left in the name of Kishore and Gayatri. Gayatri Patel asserts:

> I couldn't believe that my brother Hari, a father figure to me, could have neglected me. But I didn't say anything. What he did for the sake of the family, that was important. Personally, I thought that after making the will, he must have realized the injustice done to me, and that's why he was trying to settle me in India with my family. But it was too late.

Her nephew Uday clarified this, saying:

> My uncle probably didn't leave anything for my aunt because he had already given her three motels in the USA.

Meanwhile, Sanjeev's sudden death had also impacted many of his under-production films. Producer M.P. Ali's *Inspector Daku Aur Woh* with Randhir Kapoor, *Mang Sajaa Do Meri* and *Trupti* were shelved. According to Sayeeda Ali:

> Only two reels of *Inspector Daku Aur Woh* were ready. My husband decided to shelve it, but we lost lakhs of rupees in the process.

Producer Indu Bhushan and director Prakash Mehra tried to offer Sanjeev's role in *Insaan Ki Aulaad* to Sunil Dutt, who refused as he was busy with politics, and then to Manoj Kumar, whose son Kunal Goswami had an important role in the film. However, things didn't work out and *Insaan Ki Aulaad* got shelved as well.

R.K. Nayyar's *Qatl* (1986), Nitin Manmohan's *Baat Ban Jaaye* (1986) and Raman Kumar's *Rahee* (1987) were almost complete.

The producers raced to complete their respective projects and release them first. Meanwhile, K.C. Bokadia, Hrishikesh Mukherjee and Kant Kumar were trying to complete their films *Love and God*, *Namumkeen* (1988) and *Professor Ki Padosan* as well. *Do Waqat Ki Roti* (1988) was ready but there was no buyer.

R.K. Nayyar completed the patchwork of *Qatl*, and the film was done. The biggest question that remained was who was going to dub Sanjeev Kumar's lines. Many mimicry artists were auditioned at the BR Dubbing Theatre, one among them was Sudesh Bhosle.

Before beginning his career as mimicry artist, Bhosle worked as a painter, painting hoardings for movies with his father N.R. Bhosle. Years ago, he had even painted hoardings for Sanjeev Kumar's films, such as *Swarg Narak* and *Shriman Srimati*. Sudesh Bhosle remembers:

> I had done mimicry for everyone from Dilip Kumar to Amitabh Bachchan and Om Prakash to Asrani. However, to mimic Sanjeev Kumar is no easy task. Before *Qatl*, I had no idea about dubbing and I had practised copying his voice so many times that at one point I lost my own voice. Somehow, I got selected by Nayyar Sahib.

R.K. Nayyar handed the script to Bhosle and explained that he had to synchronize his voice with Sanjeev Kumar's lip movements. While Bhosle got the hang of his job, Sadhana Nayyar, who had just entered the theatre and could only hear Bhosle, briefly forgot that Sanjeev was no more. She exclaimed:

> Sanjeev has come on time?

Sudesh Bhosle recalls:

> When she realized her mistake she could not control her tears and immediately left the dubbing theatre.

After a week, R.K. Nayyar invited a group of journalists to his place in Santa Cruz to introduce Sudesh Bhosle to them. Again, Sadhana Nayyar looked at him and wept, reminded of Sanjeev. On 31 January 1986, *Qatl* became the first film to be released after Sanjeev Kumar's passing.

Sanjeev's friend Shatrughan Sinha, who never missed his marriage anniversary celebrations, didn't observe the occasion the following year because it fell on Sanjeev's birthday: 9 July. In Surat, Mayor Qadir Peerzada proposed naming a road after Sanjeev Kumar. After many arguments, Galemandi Main Road came to be known as Sanjeev Kumar Road. In 1988–9, Sunil Dutt inaugurated the road in the presence of the Jariwala family and the mayor. Besides this, Qadir Peerzada proposed naming a school in Surat's municipal corporation after Sanjeev Kumar and, in the 1990s, Prathamic Shala No. 123 at Nagori Wad, Sayyed Pura, Surat, came to be known as Shri Sanjeev Kumar Prathamic Shala.

The Academy of Cultural Activities and Art Institute wished to erect a statue of Sanjeev Kumar, but the Surat Mahanagar Palika couldn't provide the space. The academy then demanded an auditorium in his honour. After many a controversy, the Surat Mahanagar Palika agreed to provide the land opposite Annapurna Mandir near Rajhari's Complex. Chairman Rupin Pachigar inaugurated the construction of the auditorium in November 2009 in the presence of Sanjeev Kumar's relative Chirag Jariwala.

The academy also introduced an award in Sanjeev Kumar's name and, in 2004, the first Sanjeev Kumar Trophy was given to Abbas Mastan for Best Director. In 2013, the central government released a five-rupee postal stamp in Sanjeev Kumar's memory. The stamp bears three pictures of him, two of which are from his films *Sholay* and *Nauker*.

In December 2013, the Sanjeev Kumar Auditorium was ready. According to reports, it had cost Rs 20 crore to build, and boasts 1110 seats, six make-up rooms, two rehearsal rooms, a garden and a parking space. On 14 February 2014, the auditorium was inaugurated by the then chief minister of Gujarat (soon-to-be prime minister of India) Narendra Modi in the presence of Mayor Niranjan Zonzmera and cabinet ministers Anandiben Patel and Nanubhai Vanani, and member of Parliament Darshanaben Jardosh.

On this occasion, Uday Jariwala, Prithvi Jariwala and Chirag Jariwala handed over all of Sanjeev's trophies and awards to the state government. Today, his trophies can be found in the auditorium's lobby, open for public viewing. In his inaugural speech, Narendra Modi said:

> Sanjeev Kumar was a great actor, the pride of Gujarat. When the news of how we built an auditorium to honour him reaches Mumbai, the film industry will be greatly surprised and they will also realize that this is the way Gujarat felicitates its heroes. Yes, this took time but even after so many years of his demise he still remains in Gujarat's heart.

Around the same time Surat's municipal commissioner M.K. Das advised Sanjeev's nephew Uday to start an NGO in Sanjeev Kumar's name and Uday really liked the idea. He discussed it with his mother, Jyoti Jariwala, and on Sanjeev Kumar's seventy-sixth birthday, 9 July 2014, the SK Foundation was registered. Uday Jariwala became the founding member and seven trustees—Jyoti Jariwala, Ekta, Qadeer Peerzada, D.C. Gandhi, Neelam Jaiswal, Vikram Bhai Jariwala and Prithvi Jariwala—were appointed. The motive of the SK Foundation was to promote education, health care, culture, environment and nutrition. The foundation's first programme was held on 4 January 2015 in Surat, where free dental and eye check-ups were provided to 500 people, and within a couple of days forty patients had their cataract operation done for free. A blood donation programme was organized as well.

The SK Foundation also provided jobs to unemployed women by hiring them to make pickles, papad, farsan and other home-made items for the foundation. Whatever profit they made by selling these were used by the foundation for a good cause. The foundation also decided to give awards to upcoming Gujarati stage artistes in order to support and encourage them.

21

Love and God: Art vs Fate

Sanjeev Kumar was extremely dedicated to K. Asif's dream project, *Love and God*. He had refused many a lucrative offer for this film, wishing to stay focused on the epic project. From making lifestyle changes to distancing himself from his family, he had left no stone unturned. However, before the film could reach anywhere near completion, Sanjeev's friend and the director of this mammoth venture, K. Asif, passed away. *Love and God* suddenly became a quest. No longer just a film, it was a mission to compete with destiny, a mortal pursuit to create what was doomed since day one. In a 1974 radio interview with Ameen Sayani, Sanjeev Kumar said:

> Ameen Bhai, had Asif Sahib had the chance, he would have made films for another two hundred years. He had dreamt of making movies on the Mahabharat, Ramayana and Taj Mahal. Everything is a mess now.

After Asif passed away, Sanjeev did not give up on *Love and God*. He met Dilip Kumar a number of times and discussed the film with him. He felt that Dilip Kumar could guide this film to completion, having worked with Asif in *Mughal-E-Azam* and also as Asif's brother-in-law.

Sanjeev Kumar also approached some producers. K.C. Bokadia, who had made *Rivaaz* (1972) with Sanjeev, was a big fan of K. Asif. He had even featured Asif's name in the credits of *Rivaaz* as a well-wisher. However, when Sanjeev approached Bokadia with this ambitious project, the producer's career was still at a nascent stage and he was ill-equipped to take up a project of this magnitude. He promised Sanjeev that he would keep *Love and God* in mind and, once he had accumulated enough funds, would take up this project.

Days turned into months and months into years, and finally, in the 1980s, having made superhit movies like *Pyar Jhukta Nahin* and *Teri Meharbaniyan*, Bokadia became one of the most successful producers in Bombay. Not having forgotten his promise, he approached Sanjeev Kumar and Asif's wife to discuss the future of *Love and God*. The rush prints of negatives they collected were not in a good condition, but they were still hopeful of finding a solution.

Bokadia realized that completing *Love and God* was going to be a costly affair, so he spoke to Gulshan Kumar, owner of T-Series, and a special screening of *Love and God*'s rush prints was arranged. Gulshan Kumar, Bokadia, Sanjeev Kumar, Jamnadas, Sudarshan Nag, Akhtar Bi and others gathered to watch the incomplete version of *Love and God*. Gulshan Kumar was not impressed, but Bokadia insisted that it was Asif's film and people would flock to the theatres because of his name. Sudarshan Nag contradicted him saying:

> Everyone comes to watch the movie on the first day because of the names associated with it, but no one comes thereafter.

However, Bokadia's luck held out, and, after *Pyar Jhukta Nahin*'s unprecedented success, T-Series came into the spotlight and Gulshan Kumar decided to review *Love and God*.

After fourteen years, the shooting for the film began once again. A set of a *tehkhana* was created by art director M.K. Sayyed at Chandivali studio and the chief assistant director, Baldeo Pal, picturized some scenes here on Sanjeev Kumar with the help of cameraman R.D. Mathur. Apart from shooting, Sanjeev also began to dub at the BR Dubbing Theatre and the last dialogue he dubbed was: '*Maine Namaaz ada karli hai Laila ke daman par.*'

Dilip Kumar and Saira Banu came to bless Mrs Akhtar Asif and Sanjeev Kumar at the dubbing studio. But nothing could save this film from its fate. Within a couple of days of shooting, Sanjeev's health began to deteriorate and just like Guru Dutt and K. Asif, he too passed away leaving this project incomplete.

Sanjeev's demise, far from discouraging Bokadia, fuelled him to complete this film at any cost. He resumed shooting with Sanjeev Kumar's body double, but no one was satisfied with the outcome and eventually everybody decided to wind it up once and for all, as by then they had exhausted all their means.

The most vital scene, which takes place in heaven, was removed from the final cut and the editors decided that some long and mid-shots of Guru Dutt had to remain. So, among its many other bizarre features, both Guru Dutt and Sanjeev Kumar can be seeing playing the same part in this film.

The post-production and dubbing work soon began and many dubbing artists were called for an audition by Akhtar Bi. Sudesh Bhosle, who had already lent his voice in Sanjeev Kumar's *Qatl*, had also come for the audition. But Akhtar Bi did not know about Bhosle's part in *Qatl* and when she met him, she said:

I don't think you can dub for Sanjeev; you are a Maharashtrian and our script is in Urdu; you won't be able to do justice to this language.

According to Sudesh Bhosle:

At this point one gentleman advised me not to dub for *Love and God* because, according to him, this film was jinxed and whoever worked for this film died soon. But I disagreed and gave the audition and I was selected to dub for Sanjeev Kumar.

The film, against all these insurmountable odds, finally released but, as was expected, flopped at the box office. Nobody could believe that this was a K. Asif creation. Writer Javed Siddiqui said:

> The way *Love and God* was made was not ideal and we saw the film in pieces. Somewhere we saw Guru Dutt and somewhere Sanjeev Kumar. It was a very bad experience. I could not believe the film which was shown could be a creation of K. Asif Sahib.

The fact that *Love and God* had even made it to the theatres, despite the formidable trials, challenges and even sudden deaths that punctuated its course, was an incredible feat in itself. The film was not made for commercial success. It was an example of how the industry back then would come together for a cause and support a fellow artist's dream even when he was no longer by their side. And even though neither the director nor any of the lead actors were alive when the film released, they had won their battle against Fate. *Love and God* remains one of the most mysterious and terrifyingly fascinating movies ever made.

22

The Last Movie: *Professor Ki Padosan*

Making a film is nothing less than a gamble. Producers who invest in all the right 'ingredients' are often left baffled when the movie falls flat on its face at the box office. Then there are times when the venture is doomed from the word go, like in the case of K. Asif's *Love and God*. In spite of all the planning that goes into the making of a film, innumerable things can go wrong. One such venture was Kant Kumar's *Professor Ki Padosan*, which would not be released until 1994, even though the film was announced in 1981.

The idea of making *Professor Ki Padosan* struck Kant Kumar after witnessing the roaring success of B.R. Chopra's *Pati Patni Aur Woh*. Kumar wasn't new to the industry, having worked as an assistant to director Jagdish Gautam in *Tipu Sultan* (1959), Mandi Burman in *Manzil* (1960), Vishram Bedekar in *Rustam Sohrab* (1963), and also having produced *Bank Robbery* (1969) and *Dhongee* (1979) in the past.

When Kumar decided to produce *Professor Ki Padosan*, he signed Ravi Tandon primarily because Tandon shared a good rapport with Sanjeev Kumar, an actor he was desperate to cast. Ravi Tandon, knowing Sanjeev's busy schedule, suggested to Kant Kumar that he cast Dharmendra in the lead, but Kant Kumar wouldn't have it any other way. It had to be a Sanjeev Kumar and Padmini Kolhapure starrer. Sanjeev was an indelible part of his vision, having brilliantly portrayed the role of the erring husband in *Pati Patni Aur Woh*, and Kolhapure was Kant Kumar's real-life *padosan* (neighbour).

Since both Sanjeev and Tandon were busy, it was not until 21 January 1983 that the film was launched at Juhu in a palatial bungalow. Even after it went on the floors, the shoot was staggered because the artistes could hardly provide dates. As a result, only 40 per cent of the film was completed after a year and a half of shooting. The funds were sufficient, but some problem or the other would continually crop up with Sanjeev Kumar and he would have to cancel his shoot.

Sanjeev lost his younger brother, Nikul, and then his own health began deteriorating. Despite all the seemingly insurmountable challenges, Sanjeev still moved heaven and earth in a bid to complete *Professor Ki Padosan*. However, sometimes that is not enough. When he returned after his surgery, looking markedly frailer and weaker, the stark change in his appearance made Kant Kumar decide that it would be best to allow Sanjeev time to recuperate and return to the set healthier; but destiny had other cruel plans.

After Sanjeev Kumar's untimely demise, the producer was in big trouble. He could neither complete the movie nor could he shelve it at this late stage because that would mean bankruptcy. Film-maker Manmohan Desai had promised Kant Kumar any help he needed, including starting a new film for him. Kant Kumar joined hands with Ketan Desai, Manmohan's Desai's son, and organized a trial show of the incomplete film *Professor Ki Padosan* at a preview theatre. The show was sponsored by the IMPPA's funds, and, apart from the Desais, Ramraj Nahta, B.K. Adarsh, Anil Ganguli, Surendra Mohan, Sudarshan Nag, Pranlal Mehta, Kishore Jariwala and Ravi Tandon were also present. After carefully viewing the rush prints and going over a couple of scenes again, the producers and directors gathered for a discussion at the IMPPA office the very next day.

Director Anil Ganguly came up with a creative solution, that instead of putting more money into this film, the existing version could be edited and released. The story could be narrated in the background with a voiceover by Ameen Sayani, sketches of the characters could be made to further the plot and, in the end, a part of Sanjeev Kumar's funeral along with the tributes paid by other film stars could be shown to justify the circumstances which led to the film being made this way.

Surendra Mohan and Pranlal Mehta also advised the producer not to invest any more money in this project, and B.K. Adarsh took this opportunity to suggest that the film be released without further ado while the death of Sanjeev was still fresh in the audience's mind.

After listening to everyone, Manmohan Desai came up with an even more bizarre solution, which he claimed could turn out to be ingenious if executed correctly. He insisted that nothing was impossible or incredible in the world of cinema and, if Sanjeev Kumar's character Vidyadhar could be made invisible on screen, all these niggling issues could be sorted out. Producer Kant Kumar took this suggestion well but the captain of this ship, Ravi Tandon, was not in favour of this weird twist. He held his tongue while the discussions were on because everyone seemed to be onboard with Desai, and he quietly left the room—ironically, turning himself invisible from *Professor Ki Padosan*.

Kant Kumar now had to get down to business with writer Rajesh Majumdar, making a fresh new script with a few more scenes picturing Vidyadhar, taken in long and mid-shots, with Kishore Jariwala playing his body double. Tragically, however, Kishore passed away as well, before the shooting could begin. Majumdar found himself rewriting the script of this ill-fated venture; this time he created two more characters, played by Shekhar Suman and Vasant Sena, to help the plot move forward.

Majumdar took almost seven months to pen the story, and by August 1986 a bound script was ready for shooting when, out of the blue, news arrived that the lead actress Padmini Kolhapure had secretly married her boyfriend Pradeep Sharma on 13 August 1986, against the wishes of her parents. Poonam Dhillon, Jeetendra, Shobha Kapoor and Shakti Kapoor were present during the ceremony. After tying the knot, the newly-weds had left for Jaipur to take the grooms parents' blessing and would next head to London for their honeymoon. Kant Kumar was neither aware of nor invited to this wedding. According to Kant Kumar:

> In my case, there was always trouble. When I was planning to make *Dhongee*, I decided to cast Dimple Kapadia but, before I could begin, she married Rajesh Khanna. My second choice was Jaya Bhaduri but when I approached her secretary Sushma Kamat I found out that she too was getting married to Amitabh Bachchan. At last I began the film with Neetu Singh but before the release, she also got married to Rishi Kapoor.

As soon as the news of Kolhapure's marriage spread, all of a sudden film financiers and distributors lost interest in *Professor Ki Padosan*. Kumar was still not ready to shelve this film, having faith in its value as Sanjeev Kumar's last film. Manmohan Desai assured Kumar that he would convince Amitabh Bachchan to lend his voice as a narrator and the inclusion of the mega star's voice would be enough to find distributors for the film. However, when Kumar approached director Ravi Tandon with the new script, Ravi refused to be a part of *Professor Ki Padosan*. According to Ravi Tandon:

> I went through the script, but the subject was no longer to my taste; a lot of trick photography was required, so I politely refused without asking for my balance amount. I gave a no-objection certificate to the producer to sign any director. I even suggested director Babubhai Mistry who was a master in trick photography and the producer agreed to my point of view.

As advised by Tandon, Kumar approached director Babubhai Mistry, who was busy shooting Manoj Kumar's film *Kalyug Aur Ramayan* (1987). Only after a lot of convincing did he agree to complete *Professor Ki Padosan*, but the deal-breaker was that he said he would need sixty shifts to complete the shoot. The producer was not in a position to invest that amount of money. Kant Kumar's venture had taken a *Love and God* turn and the general opinion was that this project was doomed. Kumar was also regretting his decision of not shooting with Sanjeev, while the other producers had perhaps foreseen the oncoming tragedy and shot as much as they could while Sanjeev was still around.

In this hour of darkness, director Shantilal Soni stepped up to help complete *Professor Ki Padosan* without any strings attached and within the given budget. All the artistes, including Asha Parekh, Padmini Kolhapure, Shoma Anand and Dinesh Hingoo, agreed to cooperate with Kant Kumar. The producer's friend and a huge fan of Sanjeev Kumar, Ramesh Tela, helped him financially when no financier was ready to lend him money and the shooting began after a gap of six years. Miraculously, this time, the film was finally completed.

Sanjeev Kumar's friend B.R. Ishara came forward to complete the post-production work without taking a fee. However, there was still no buyer for this controversial film. Manmohan Desai contacted Amitabh Bachchan as planned and asked him to lend his voice as a narrator. Bachchan, who always considered Sanjeev a dear friend and had worked with Desai in superhit ventures like *Amar Akbar Anthony, Coolie* and *Mard*, not only agreed to narrate a prologue, but also suggested doing so facing the camera to increase the impact of his presence. Amitabh Bachchan, who didn't even know Kant Kumar, agreed to do all of this free of cost.

Now that Amitabh Bachchan's name was associated with this film, distributors began to show a keen interest in the project. Soon dubbing began and this time, there was no doubt as to who would dub Sanjeev Kumar's voice. Sudesh Bhosle had already proven his mettle by dubbing for Sanjeev in *Qatl* and *Love and God,* and he would lend his voice to *Professor Ki Padosan* as well. Incredible as it may sound, the movie, Sanjeev Kumar's last onscreen presence, released in 1994, almost nine years after his death.

Awards Won by Sanjeev Kumar

1) Best Maharashtra Stage Actor Award for the Gujarati play *Koi No Ladak Vayo* in Mumbai.

2) Naval Stars Award, 1969 (Shanoo Varun Trophy by S.M. Nanda).

3) Filmfare Award for Best Supporting Actor for *Shikar*, 1968.

4) Eighteenth National Awards, Best Actor Award—presented by the deputy information and broadcasting minister Nandini Satapthi—for *Dastak*, 1970.

5) Surat Jilla Leuva Patidar Gnyati on 4 April 1971 in Surat, Gujarat.

6) Twentieth National Awards, Best Actor Award for *Koshish*, 1972.

7) Bengal Film Journalists' Association Best Actor Award for *Koshish*, 1974.

8) Best Actor Award by Uttar Pradesh Patrakar Sangh for *Mausam*, 1975.

9) Cinegoers Council (Delhi) Award, 1975.

10) Lions Club of North Calcutta, Actor of the Year Award for *Mausam*, 1975.

11) Filmfare Award for Best Actor for *Aandhi*, 1975.

12) Filmfare Award for Best Actor for *Arjun Pandit*, 1976.
13) Army Officers Voice Association Trophy.
14) Chitralok Cine Serjak Award in Ahmedabad.
15) Maratha Seva Sangh, Best Actor Award in Khed, Maharashtra, on 2 April 1984.
16) Kalashri Art and Network, Lifetime Achievement Millennium 2000 Award, in Surat, Gujarat.

Filmography

1. *Hum Hindustani*
1960
Director: Ram Mukherjee
(Remake of Nirmla De's 1952 Bengali film *Basu Paribar*.)

2. *Aao Pyar Karein*
1964
Director: R.K. Nayyar
(In the credits, Sanjeev Kumar and Mac Mohan were introduced as Sanjay and Brij Mohan respectively.)

3. *Nishan*
1965
Director: Aspi Irani
(Harihar Jariwala was introduced as Sanjeev Kumar.)

4. *Husn Aur Ishq*
1966
Director: Naresh Kumar

5. *Smuggler*
1966
Director: Aspi Irani

6. *Pati Patni*
1966
Director: S.A. Akbar

7. *Alibaba Aur 40 Chor*
1966
Director: Homi Wadia

8. *Badal*
1966
Director: Aspi Irani

9. *Aayega Aanewala*
1967
Director: Kewal Mishra

10. *Gunehgaar*
1967
Director: R. Thakkar

11. *Naunihal*
1967
Director: Raj Marbros

12. *Saathi*
1968
Director: Sridhar

13. *Shikaar*
1968
Director: Atmaram
(Winner at 16th Filmfare Awards, Best Supporting Actor.)

14. *Sunghursh*
1968
Director: H.S. Rawail

15. *Raja Aur Runk*
1968
Director: K.P. Atma

16. *Gauri*
1969
Director: A. Bhim Singh
(Sivaji Ganesan was so impressed working for producer A.L. Srinivasan's Tamil film *Shanti* in 1965 with actress Devika that he decided to produce its Hindi remake, *Gauri*.)

17. *Jyoti*
1969
Director: Dulal Guha

18. *Anokhi Raat*
1969
Director: Asit Sen

19. *Aashirwad*
1969
Director: Hrishikesh Mukherjee

20. *Jeene Ki Raah*
1969
Director: L.V. Prasad

21. *Dharti Kahe Pukar Ke*
1969
Director: Dulal Guha

22. *Chanda Aur Bijlee*
1969
Director: Atmaram

23. *Sachaai*
1969
Director: K. Shanker

24. *Satyakam*
1970
Director: Hrishikesh Mukherjee

25. *Bandhan*
1970
Director: Narendra Bedi

26. *Insaan Aur Shaitan*
1970
Director: Aspi Irani

27. *Khilona*
1970
Director: Chander Vora
(Nominated for Best Actor at the 18th Filmfare Awards; Rajesh Khanna won for *Sachcha Jhootha*. The film was based on Gulshan Nanda's novel *Patthar Ke Honth*. A remake of Gujarati film *Mare Jau Pahle Par*, which was also based on *Patthar Ke Honth*.)

28. *Insaaf Ka Mandir*
1970
Director: B.R. Ishara

29. *Maa Ka Aanchal*
1970
Director: Jagdeo Bhamri

30. *Gunaah Aur Kanoon*
1970
Director: B.R. Ishara

31. *Dastak*
1970
Director: Rajinder Singh Bedi
(Winner of National Award for Best Actor.)

32. *Gustakhi Maaf*
1970
Director: Raj Kumar Bedi

33. *Oos Raat Ke Baad*
1970
Director: Y.B. Siraj

34. *Bachpan*
1970
Director: K.P. Atma

35. *A Night in Calcutta*
1970
Director: Amrit Mahendra

36. *Priya*
1970
Director: Govind Saraiya

37. *Devi*
1970
Director: V. Madhusudhan Rao

38. *Umang*
1971
Director: Atmaram

39. *Ek Paheli*
1971
Director: Naresh Kumar

40. *Paras*
1971
Director: C.P. Dixit

41. *Man Mandir*
1971
Director: Chanakya

42. *Purani Pehchan*
1971
Director: Kewal Mishra

43. *Anubhav*
1971
Director: Basu Bhattacharya
(Winner of National Film Award for Best Feature Film.)

44. *Kangan*
1972
Director: K.B. Tilak

45. *Rivaaj*
1972
Director: T. Prakash Rao

46. *Subah-O-Shaam*
1972
Director: Chanakya
(First Indian film to be shot in Iran with Iranian actors.)

47. *Jai Jwala*
1972
Director: Manohar Deepak
(The film re-released on 14 March 1980 with the new title *Puja Aur Payal*)

48. *Parichay*
1972
Director: Gulzar

49. *Seeta Aur Geeta*
1972
Director: Ramesh Sippy

50. *Sabse Bada Sukh*
1972
Director: Hrishikesh Mukherjee

51. *Koshish*
1972
Director: Gulzar
(Winner of National Award for Best Actor for the year 1973. Winner of Bombay Film Journalist Association Award for Best Actor. Nominated for Best Actor at the 20th Filmfare Awards; Manoj Kumar won for *Be-Imaan*. The Tamil film *Vyarandhavargal* (1977)

was a remake of *Koshish*. It was directed by T.N. Balu, with Kamal
Haasan and Sujatha in the leads.)

52. *Rocky Mera Naam*
1973
Director: Sataram Rohara

53. *Anamika*
1973
Director: Raghunath Jhalani

54. *Suraj Aur Chanda*
1973
Director: T. Madhavrao

55. *Anhonee*
1973
Director: Ravi Tandon

56. *Archana*
1973
Director: Satpal

57. *Manchali*
1974
Director: Raja Nawathe

58. *Dawat*
1974
Director: B.R. Ishara

59. *Manoranjan*
1974
Director: Shammi Kapoor

60. *Agni Rekha*
1974
Director: Mahesh Kaul
(Mahesh Kaul passed away during the filming. The film was completed by Hrishikesh Mukherjee.)

61. *Aap Ki Kasam*
1974
Director: J. Om Prakash
(Remake of K.S. Sethumadhavan's 1970 Malayalam film *Vazhve Mayam*.)

62. *Naya Din Nayee Raat*
1974
Director: A. Bhim Singh
(Remake of A.P. Nagarajan's 1964 Tamil film *Navarathri*.)

63. *Chowkidaar*
1974
Director: Shyam Ralhan

64. *Door Nahin Manzil*
1974
Director: Hari Walia

65. *Shandaar*
1974
Director: Krishnan Panju

66. *Kunwara Baap*
1974
Director: Mehmood

67. *Charitraheen*
1974
Director: Shakti Samanta

68. *Imaan*
1975
Director: Padmanath

69. *Aandhi*
1975
Director: Gulzar
(Winner at the 23rd Filmfare Awards, for Best Actor.)

70. *Apne Rang Hazar*
1975
Director: Ravi Tandon

71. *Aakraman*
1975
Director: J. Om Prakash

72. *Dhoti Lota Aur Chowpatty*
1975
Director: Mohan Choti

73. *Sholay*
1975
Director: Ramesh Sippy
(Nominated for Best Actor at the 23rd Filmfare Awards; he won it
for *Aandhi*.)

74. *Uljhan*
1975
Director: Raghunath Jhalani

75. *Faraar*
1975
Director: Shankar Mukherjee

76. *Mausam*
1975
Director: Gulzar
(Nominated for Best Actor at the 24th Filmfare Awards. Sanjeev Kumar won the award for *Arjun Pandit*.)

77. *Apne Dushman*
1976
Director: Kailash Bhandari

78. *Vishwasghat*
1976
Director: Mahesh Bhatt

79. *Arjun Pandit*
1976
Director: Hrishikesh Mukherjee
(Winner of Best Actor at the 24th Filmfare Awards.)

80. *Imaan Dharam*
1977
Director: Desh Mukherjee

81. *Zindagi*
1977
Director: Ravi Tandon

82. *Paapi*
1977
Director: O.P. Ralhan

83. *Mukti*
1977
Director: Raj Tilak

84. *Yahi Hai Zindagi*
1977
Director: K.S. Sethumadhavan
(Nominated for Best Actor at the 25th Filmfare Awards; the award
went to Amitabh Bachchan for *Amar Akbar Anthony.*)

85. *Alaap*
1977
Director: Hrishikesh Mukherjee

86. *Dhoop Chhaon*
1977
Director: Prahlad Sharma

87. *Angarey*
1977
Director: Govind Saraiya

88. *Do Ladkiyan*
1977
Director: K.P. Atma

89. *Dil Aur Patthar*
1977
Director: Kanak Mishra

90. *Apnapan*
1978
Director: J. Om Prakash

91. *Tumhare Liye*
1978
Director: Basu Chatterjee

92. *Saawan Ke Geet*
1978
Director: Ratan Bhattacharya

93. *Trishul*
1978
Director: Yash Chopra
(Nominated for Best Supporting Actor at the 26th Filmfare Awards;
the award went to Saeed Jaffrey for *Shatranj Ke Khilari*.)

94. *Pati Patni Aur Woh*
1978
Director: B.R. Chopra
(Nominated for Best Actor at the 26th Filmfare Awards; the award
went to Amitabh Bachchan for *Don*.)

95. *Muqaddar*
1978
Director: Ravi Tandon

96. *Trishna*
1978
Director: Anil Ganguly

97. *Shatranj Ke Khilari*
1978
Director: Satyajit Ray

98. *Devta*
1978
Director: S. Ramanathan
(Nominated for Best Actor at the 26th Filmfare Awards; the award
went to Amitabh Bachchan for *Don.*)

99. *Swarg Narak*
1978
Director: Daseri Narayana Rao

100. *Humare Tumhare*
1979
Director: Umesh Mehra

101. *Inspector Eagle*
1979
Director: Vishwamitter Adil

102. *Maan Apmaan*
1979
Director: N.V. Deshpande

103. *Jaani Dushman*
1979
Director: Rajkumar Kohli

104. *Kaala Patthar*
1979
Director: Yash Chopra

105. *Ghar Ki Laaj*
1979
Director: B.R. Ishara

106. *Bombay by Night*
1979
Director: A. Shamsheer

107. *Nauker*
1979
Director: Ismail Memon
(Ismail Memon passed away during the making of the film; it was completed by Jyoti Swaroop.)

108. *Takkar*
1980
Director: K. Bapaiah

109. *Swayamvar*
1980
Director: P. Sambasiva Rao

110. *Jyoti Bane Jwala*
1980
Director: Dasari Narayana Rao

111. *Be-Reham*
1980
Director: Raghunath Jhalani

112. *Abdullah*
1980
Director: Sanjay Khan

113. *Patthar Se Takkar*
1980
Director: Gulab Mehta

114. *Hum Paanch*
1981
Director: Bapu

115. *Waqt Ki Deewar*
1981
Director: Ravi Tandon

116. *Chehre Pe Chehra*
1981
Director: Raj Tilak

117. *Ladies Tailor*
1981
Director: Khalid Akhtar

118. *Biwi O Biwi*
1981
Director: Rahul Rawail

119. *Itni Si Baat*
1981
Director: Madhu M.

120. *Daasi*
1981
Director: Raj Khosla

121. *Silsila*
1981
Director: Yash Chopra

122. *Griha Pravesh*
1981
Director: Basu Bhattacharya

123. *Hathkadi*
1982
Director: Surendra Mohan

124. *Angoor*
1982
Director: Gulzar
(Nominated for Best Actor at the 30th Filmfare Awards; the award
went to Dilip Kumar for *Shakti*.)

125. *Shriman Shrimati*
1982
Director: Vijaya Reddy

126. *Sindoor Bane Jwala*
1982
Director: K. Bapaiah

127. *Suraag*
1982
Director: Jagmohan Mundra

128. *Namkeen*
1982
Director: Gulzar

129. *Ayaash*
1982
Director: Shakti Samanta

130. *Sawaal*
1982
Director: Ramesh Talwar

131. *Khuddar*
1982
Director: Ravi Tandon

132. *Vidhaata*
1982
Director: Subhash Ghai
(Nominated for Best Supporting Actor at 30th Filmfare Awards; the award went to Shammi Kapoor for the same film.)

133. *Log Kya Kahenge*
1983
Director: B.R. Ishara

134. *Hero*
1983
Director: Subhash Ghai

135. *Mera Dost Mera Dushman*
1984
Director: Raj Khosla

136. *Pakhandee*
1984
Director: Sameer Ganguly

137. *Yaadgar*
1984
Director: Dasari Narayana Rao

138. *Lakhon Ki Baat*
1984
Director: Basu Chatterjee

139. *Haathon Ki Lakiren*
1984
Director: Chetan Anand

140. *Ram Tere Kitne Naam*
1985
Director: P. Madhavan

141. *Bad Aur Badnaam*
1985
Director: Feroz Chinoy

142. *Chhota Aadmi*
1985
Director: Krishnakant

143. *Zabardast*
1985
Director: Nasir Hussain

144. *Rusvaai*
1985
Director: Rajat Rakshit
(The film re-released in 1991 with the new title *Nishani*.)

145. *Kanch Ki Deewar*
1986
Director: M.N. Yasin

146. *Qatl*
1986
Director: R.K. Nayyar

147. *Baat Ban Jaaye*
1986
Director: Bharat Rangachary

148. *Love and God*
1986
Director: K. Asif

149. *Badkaar*
1987
Director: Shiv Kumar

150. *Rahee*
1987
Director: Raman Kumar

151. *Hirasat*
1987
Director: Surendra Mohan

152. *Do Waqt Ki Roti*
1988
Director: Satpal

153. *Namumkin*
1988
Director: Hrishikesh Mukherjee

154. *Oonch Neech Beech*
1989
Director: Wasi Khan

155. *Professor Ki Padosan*
1994
Director: Shantilal Soni

NON-HINDI FILMS

1. *Ramat Ramade Ram* (Gujarati)
1964
Director: Dinesh Rawal

2. *Kalaapi* (Gujarati)
1966
Director: Manhar Raskapur

3. *Mare Jaau Pehle Paar* (Gujarati)
1968
Director: Chandrakant Sangani

4. *Jigar Ane Ami* (Gujarati)
1970
Director: Chandrakant Sangani

5. *Donhi Gharcha Pahuna* (Marathi)
1971
Director: Gajanan Jagirdar

6. *Bharatha Vilas* (Tamil)
1973
Director: A.C. Trilogchander

7. *Urvashi* (Telugu)
1974
Director: Tiptur Raghu

8. *Hojamaalo* (Sindhi)
1979
Director: Rajan Chawla

9. *Udeekan* **(Punjabi)**
1979
Director: Haridutt Sharma

10. *Fauji Chacha* **(Punjabi)**
1980
Director: Mohan Bhakhri

11. *Bijlee* **(Marathi)**
1986
Director: Anant Marathe

Interviews Conducted by the Authors[*]

1) A.K. Hangal, 16 February 2010, at his residence, Santa Cruz, Mumbai.

2) Javed Khan, 21 February 2010, at his residence, Kandivali, Mumbai.

3) Ramesh Talwar, 3 March 2010, at his office, Link Road, Andheri, Mumbai.

4) Shammi, 17 March 2010, at her residence, Juhu, Mumbai.

5) Ruby Aspi Irani, 12 December 2010, at her residence, Nepean Sea Road, Mumbai.

6) Vidya Sinha, 14 January 2011, at her residence, Versova, Mumbai.

7) Prem Chopra, 16 January 2011, at Nibana Pali Hill, Bandra, Mumbai.

8) Deven Verma, 27 January 2011, at Jeevan Nagar, Pune.

9) Nargis Irani, 30 January 2011 and 13 November 2012, at her residence, Nepean Sea Road, Mumbai.

10) Deepak Balraj Vij, 2 February 2011, at his office in Mumbai.

---

[*] Please note that only relevant information from the interviews has been used in the book.

11) Subhash Indori, 10 February 2011, at Carter Road Restaurant, Mumbai.

12) J. Omprakash, 16 February 2011, at Filmkraft office, Link Road, Andheri, Mumbai.

13) Geeta Siddharth, 3 March 2011, at her residence, Movie Tower, Lokhandwala, Andheri, Mumbai.

14) Anil Ganguly, 11 March 2011, at his residence, Worli, Mumbai.

15) Dilip Kumar, 11 April 2011, 19 October 2011 and 13 December 2012, at his bungalow, Pali Hill, Mumbai.

16) Ravi Tandon, 17 April 2011 and 15 May 2011, at Tandon House, Juhu, Mumbai.

17) B R Ishara, 24 April 2011 and 9 November 2012, at his residence.

18) Rehana Sultan, 29 April 2011, 9 November 2012 and 16 September, at her residence, Juhu, Mumbai.

19) Rohidas Bangera, 3 May 2011, at CP Tank, Mumbai.

20) Ahsan Khan, 5 May 2011, in Bandra, near Holy Family Hospital, Mumbai.

21) Aslam Khan, 5 May 2011, in Bandra, near Holy Family Hospital, Mumbai.

22) Master Bittu, 19 May 2011, at B.R. Chopra's office, 15th Road, Khar, Mumbai.

23) Sudhir Dalvi, 21 May 2011, at dubbing theatre, Veera Desai Road, Mumbai.

24) Raman Kumar, 25 May 2011, at his office, Link Road, Andheri, Mumbai.

25) Hema Dewdekar, 27 May 2011, at Tank Bldg, Bhuleshwar, Mumbai.

26) Parikshit Sahni, 29 May 2011, at his residence, Juhu, Mumbai.

27) Prakash Kapoor, 30 May 2011, at Infinity Mall, Andheri, Mumbai.

28) C.H. Intwala, 3 June 2011, at his Parel residence, Mumbai.

29) Basu Chatterjee, 16 June 2011, at his Santa Cruz residence, Mumbai.

30) Farida Jalal, 20 June 2011, at Indra Darshan, Oshiwara, Mumbai.

31) Mumta Satish Jariwala, 23 June 2011, at her residence, Surat, Gujarat.

32) Chandrakant Chatiyawala, 24 June 2011, at Moti Sheri, Surat, Gujarat.

33) Ramesh Babubhai Patel, 24 June 2011, in Surat, Gujarat.

34) Chirag Jariwala, 24 June 2011, in Surat, Gujarat.

35) Sagar Sarhadi, 30 June 2011, at his office, Link Road, Andheri, Mumbai.

36) Narendra Upadhyay, 6 July 2011, at Saburi Restaurant, Andheri, Mumbai.

37) Prafullah Kishore Jariwala, 9 July 2011, 27 October 2011 and 14 August 2014, her residence, near Juhu Garden, Mumbai.

38) Rohini Hattangadi, 13 July 2011, interview on phone call, Mumbai.

39) Sadhana Singh, 18 July 2011, interview on phone call, Mumbai.

40) Sudesh Bhosle, 18 July 2011, interview on phone call, Mumbai.

41) Ram Mohan, 24 July 2011, at his residence, Juhu Tara Road, Mumbai.

42) Niranjan Mehta, 27 July 2011, at his residence, Princess Street, near Juma Masjid, Mumbai.

43) Sayeedaali, 31 July 2011 and 13 December 2013, at her Marine Drive residence, Mumbai.

44) Mahesh Desai, 4 August 2011, at his Pydhonie residence, Mumbai.

45) Tarla Mehta, 12 August 2011, at her residence, Matunga, Mumbai.

46) Tarla Joshi, 14 August 2011, at her residence, Andheri, East Mumbai.

47) Padmarani, 18 August 2011, at her residence, Nepean Sea Road, Mumbai.

48) Dinesh Hingoo, 20 August 2011, at Mehboob Studio, Bandra, Mumbai.

49) Shobha Pradhan, 8 October 2011, at her residence, Bandra, East Mumbai.

50) Kailash Advani, 11 October 2011, at his residence, Mira Road, dist. Thane.

51) Arvind Joshi, 11 October 2011, at his residence, Vile Parle, Mumbai.

52) Bachchu Sampat, 19 October 2011, at her residence, Gawalia Tank, Mumbai.

53) Saroj Khan, 20 October 2011, at Satyam Hall, Juhu, Mumbai.

54) Alyque Padamsee, 23 October 2011, on phone call, Mumbai.

55) Kanan Kaushal, 6 November 2011, at her Worli residence, Mumbai.

56) Sarika, 19 December 2011, at her Carter Road residence, Mumbai.

57) Govind Saraiya, 26 December 2011, at his residence, Camps Corner, Mumbai.

58) Jyoti Jariwala, 5 January 2012 and 1 July 2012, at her residence, Parin Villa, Bandra, Mumbai.

59) Uday Jariwala, 5 January 2012 and 1 July 2012, at Parin Villa, Bandra, Mumbai.

60) Prithvi Jariwala, 5 January 2012, at Parin Villa, Bandra, Mumbai.

61) Anju Mahendru, 8 January 2012, at her residence, Mumbai.

62) Madhumati, 20 January 2012, at her residence, Juhu, Mumbai.

63) Deepak Jamnadas, 26 February 2012, at Parin Villa, Bandra, Mumbai.

64) Sulbha Arya, 1 March 2012, at her Juhu residence, Mumbai.

65) Surdarshan Naag, 24 August 2012, at his residence, Bandra, Mumbai.

66) Nayantara Pithodia, 25 August 2012, at her residence, Andheri, Mumbai.

67) Chintamani Madhavrao Pandya, 31 August 2012, at his residence, Thakurduwar, Mumbai.

68) Prabha Shah, 7 September 2012, at Parin Villa, Bandra, Mumbai.

69) Jigna Shah, 9 September 2012, at her residence, Mumbai.

70) Sachin Pilgaonkar, 30 September 2012, at his office, behind Lido Cinema, Juhu, Mumbai.

71) Javed Siddiqui, 4 October 2012, at his office, Andheri, Mumbai.

72) Imtiaz Khan, 13 October 2012, at his residence, Pali Hill, Mumbai.

73) Madan Jain, 15 October 2012, interview on phone call, Mumbai.

74) Sadhana Nayyar, 4 December 2012, at her Santa Cruz bungalow, Mumbai.

75) Sameer Ganguly, 9 February 2013, on phone call, Mumbai.

76) Kanak Jariwala, 23 February 2013, in Surat, Gujarat.

77) Arun Sharma, 25 February 2013, at AC Market, Tardeo, Mumbai.

78) Shehla Amzad Khan, 27 February 2013, at Pali Hill, Mumbai.

79) Vinay Sinha, 2 March 2013, at Citi Mall, Andheri, Mumbai.

80) Artee Kumar, 2013, interview on email.

81) Bhawna Bhatt, 8 April 2013, at Vadodara, Gujarat.

82) Jayprakash Karnataki, 15 May 2013.

83) Leena Chandavarkar, 21 May 2013, at Kishore Kumar's bungalow, Juhu Tara Road, Mumbai.

84) Ramesh Sippy, 23 May 2013, at his office, Mumbai.

85) Shaukat Kaifi, 5 June 2013, at Sagar Samrat, Juhu, Mumbai.

86) Pyarelal, 27 June 2013, at his residence, Mumbai.

87) Haridutt Sharma, 9 September 2013, interview on phone call, Mumbai.

88) Ashok Patel, 3 February 2014, at Prabha's residence, Marol Maroshi Road, Mumbai.

89) Gulzar Vishul, 25 January to 2 February 2014, interview shoot at his bungalow, Pali Hill, Mumbai. With the help of Uday Jariwala and our team, for a short documentary on Sanjeev Kumar that would be screened in Surat on 14 February 2014, during the inauguration of the Sanjeev Kumar Auditorium.

90) Gayatri Patel, 24 February 2014, at Parin Villa, Mumbai, and on 3 March 2014, at Prabha Shah's residence, Marol Maroshi Road, Mumbai.

91) Pandit, 5 March 2014, at Parin Villa, Bandra, Mumbai.

92) Ashok Saraf, 3 April 2014, at Rajkamal Studio, Parel, Mumbai.

93) Srikant Mohge, 5 April 2014, in Kondva, Pune.

94) Mushtaq Merchant, 11 April 2014, at his brother Ishtiyaq Merchant's place, Bandra, Mumbai.

95) Anjana Mumtaz, 14 May 2014, at her residence, Juhu, Mumbai.

96) Kalpana Jariwala, 5 June 2014, at her residence, Surat, Gujarat.

97) Anil Desai, 6 June 2014, in Niyode, Gujarat.

98) Harshad Desai, 6 June 2014, in Niyode, Gujarat.

99) Hansuya, 13 June 2014, interview on phone call, from Mumbai to Sarangpur.

100) Dhanji Patel, 13 June 2014, phone call, from Mumbai to Sarangpur.

101) Padma Champaklal, 13 June 2014, on phone call, from Surat to Mumbai.

102) Piyush Jariwala, 13 June 2018, on phone call, from Surat to Mumbai.

103) Ila Jariwala, 14 June 2014, interview on phone call.

104) Balkrishna Jariwala, 18 June 2014, in Surat, Gujarat.

105) Urvashi Jariwala, 1 July 2014, at her residence, Vile Parle, East Mumbai.

106) Jayshree T., 17 August 2014, at her residence, Santa Cruz, West Mumbai.

107) Nimmi, 6 September 2014, at her residence, Neha Apartments, Juhu Tara Road, Mumbai.

108) Raj N. Sippy, 13 November 2014, interview on phone call.

109) Pravin Bhatt, 26 January 2015, at his residence, Versova, Mumbai.

110) R.R. Patthak, 14 February 2015, at his office, Seven Bungalows, Mumbai.

List of Sources

1. Gautam Chintamani, *Dark Star: The Loneliness of Being Rajesh Khanna*, HarperCollins, 2015.
2. Hanif Zaveri, *Mehmood: A Man of Many Moods*, Popular Prakashan, 2005.
3. Saba Mahmood Bashir, *Gulzar's Aandhi: Insights into the Film*, HarperCollins, 2019.
4. Anupama Chopra, *Sholay: The Making of a Classic*, Viking, 2000.
5. 'Lady Nutan', Let's Talk about Bollywood, 3 June 2014, http://www.letstalkaboutbollywood.com/article-lady-nutan-123811442.html
6. *Geetmala Ki Chhaon Mein Vol. 46–50* (audio), Gaana.com, 2014, https://gaana.com/album/geetmala-ki-chhaon-mein-vol-46-50